THE HUSTLE TRAP

THE HUSTLE TRAP

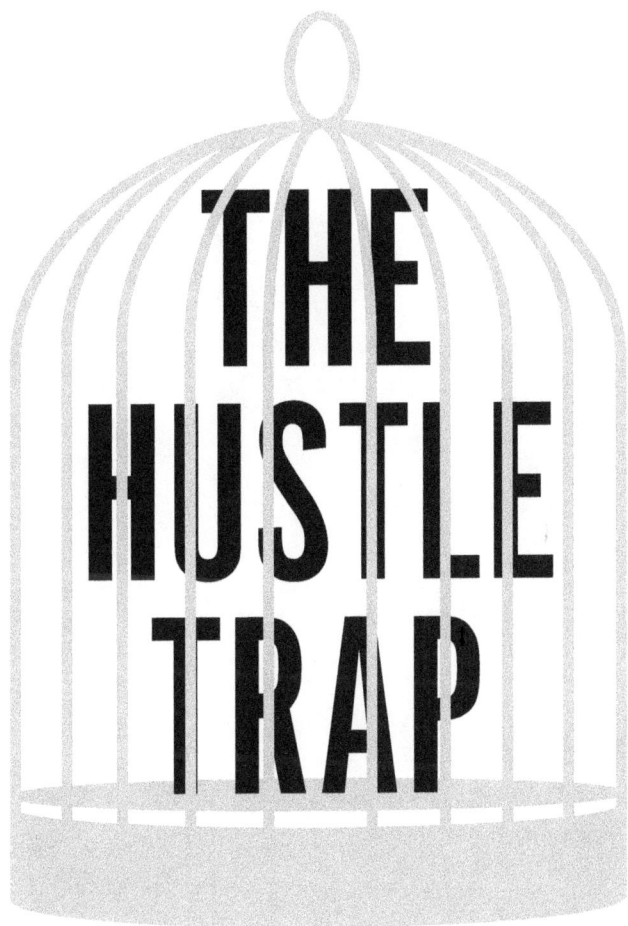

A HOW-TO GUIDE FOR DOING LESS AND MAKING MORE WITH YOUR BUSINESS

RYAN CROWNHOLM

LIONCREST
PUBLISHING

THE HUSTLE TRAP

A How-To Guide for Doing Less and Making More with Your Business

FIRST EDITION

ISBN   978-1-5445-4059-7 *Paperback*

      978-1-5445-4060-3 *Ebook*

      978-1-5445-4062-7 *Audiobook*

CONTENTS

PART 3: NEXT-LEVEL TACTICS

PART 4: LIFE ON THIS SIDE

INTRODUCTION

I'll never forget the pain.

As I rolled over and looked down, all I could see was a tangled mess of flesh and blood. My legs were no longer recognizable as legs. My upper body heaved from crushed bones and collapsed lungs. And in that moment, I did what anyone else would do: I screamed.

This particular day—July 3, 2007—started out like any other. I had put on my torn-up jeans and steel-toe boots and headed down to the first jobsite in my one-ton dually crew cab pickup, which pulled a trailer loaded with a Bobcat weighing in at 10,000 pounds. By this point, the routine was like second nature. Even though my hauling business had grown significantly, and I now had multiple trucks, multiple employees, and regular demand for our services, I still worked like I did when I first started.

This particular morning, we were unloading the equipment on a sloped street, so I was sure to check out our setup. The

Bobcat was loaded up on our 10,000 GVW flatbed trailer, as it always was, but something was off. One of the jacks, which I had welded on to keep the trailer from teetering, was missing.

"Oh, I'm not sure," Chris said, "I've been doing it with just one, and it's been fine."

I gave my okay and walked off to the side to light up a cigarette before we got started. This, too, was a routine in my day. In fact, I had smoked a pack a day since I was 15 years old, and here at 31, I was still going strong with the habit.

Little did I know what was to come next. Just as I put the cigarette out, I heard metal shift. And then CRASH!

The next thing I knew, the one-ton dually crew cab truck, with the five-ton trailer in tow, was headed straight for me. As I tried to scramble to get out of the way, my legs got tangled under me, and I fell directly in front of the oncoming truck.

This was the first, but not the last, time a simple thought crossed my mind: *my life is over.*

After the first set of wheels crushed my legs, the truck rolled over me, crushing my shoulder and tearing off my skin. Because it was so low to the ground, there was nowhere for my body to go.

As I looked up at the undercarriage of the truck, the thought occurred to me that the next thing to hit me would be the trailer jack, which was only a few inches from the ground. Once again, I had no doubt that this was, indeed, the end of my life. *This will be the final blow*, I thought.

Suddenly, I heard yet another crash. The truck had, just in the nick of time, run into another car parked down the road, and as it hit, the truck jackknifed, pulling the trailer off course.

Then, for a moment, everything was completely still.

WHAT IF YOU STOPPED?

When my world stopped, quite literally, I was forced to look at my life and business from a new perspective.

As entrepreneurs, our default is GO!

In many ways, running a business is like racing a sports car. In the beginning, things are out of control. Tires are squealing, and you're fishtailing, but as you get through the gears, the ride becomes less chaotic. Once you're in fifth gear, you're coasting, but the ultimate goal is a fully autonomous vehicle.

The problem is that many entrepreneurs get stuck in first gear and are redlining without realizing they forgot to shift.

For me, zero to one looked like running a profitable business and having the means to buy a nice house and a nice car and to even have some savings left over. Sure, I was burnt out, working harder than ever, but I figured that simply came with the territory.

In reality, I was living with a limited perspective of what was possible. I was stuck in "good enough" mode. And I had good reason for this. After all, only seven years prior, I had just gotten out of the military and had little to my name. I was at rock bottom in every sense. And here I was, a successful business-man. What more could I ask for?

Well, as it turned out, I could ask for a lot more, but not until I was forced to stop.

If you're anything like me, you're an entrepreneur because you're a fighter and dreamer. You're likely reading this book because you're always after more.

You know how to work relentlessly. Early mornings and long days are the norm. You've worn multiple hats, and you've hit some key milestones—hiring a first employee, buying new equipment, or renting a storefront.

There's only one problem: growth has not equaled less work for you. In fact, it has equaled more.

I've been there.

And I have one question: What would happen if you simply stopped—if you slammed on the brakes yourself instead of having to get run over by a truck?

Would your business go on without you? Would there be enough momentum? And more importantly, would it scale while you do even less?

FORCED TO DO LESS

As soon as the truck and trailer came to a halt, I was forced into a new reality—with one working arm.

I pulled myself from under the truck and looked down to find my left femur and right tibia sticking out of my jeans. I let out a solid scream and then clicked into my combat life-saving training, which I had learned while deployed in Bosnia in the 90s. I was in shock and wouldn't have long to live, so I started directing my employees and the customer.

"Pour some water on my lips. Put a cushion under my head. Get something to shade me. Call 911, and try to call from a landline, so they know exactly where we're at."

Finally, people were moving. And finally, I realized I might not die.

An ambulance arrived in only seven minutes, and soon enough, I was on the stretcher, with paramedics doing all they could to stop the bleeding as we headed to John Muir Medical Center. This was the most painful drive of my life. I remember thinking, *Why the fuck did they put speed bumps on the final approach to the ER?*

As I entered the hospital, a whole trauma team came to my side. Before I knew it, someone's finger was up my ass to test for internal bleeding. "Guys, I've got enough going on here," I said, trying to find any moment of lightness in the horror of it all.

Unfortunately, that was the end of any funny business; it was time for traction. As a few people held down my upper body, others pulled my legs so that the bones would go back into my skin and align to look somewhat normal again. It was, in short, medieval torture.

After they sedated me, I went straight into trauma surgery,

where I remained for eleven hours as they pieced me back together.

Then, on July 4th, I woke up confined to a hospital bed with titanium rods in both legs, labored breath from my punctured lungs, a shattered left shoulder, and a dozen tubes and wires coming out of my body.

A hospital bed was the most unnatural place for me to be. Just a couple of days before this, I was someone who enjoyed working long days full of manual labor, running miles when I got home, and staying more active than anyone I knew. How was I going to live without my physicality?

That day, a few friends showed up to check on me. When they left, I couldn't help but think they were there because it was the "right" thing to do. My girlfriend visited too, but she too didn't provide the comfort or support I needed, and I asked her not to visit again.

The following week, I had little else to do but evaluate my life. And that is exactly what I did.

It didn't take long for me to acknowledge I had built a house of cards around me. Everything I had built was superficial. And even though I had built what many would consider to be an ideal life, I had settled along the way. The friends were *good enough*. The girlfriend was *good enough*. The house was *good enough*. The business was *good enough*.

So, right then and there, I began to determine how things were going to change. My first step: quit smoking. This was one thing

I could control, so I committed to the change. Sure enough, I never smoked another cigarette again.

This single decision set me on a path—to stop making excuses, to stop settling, and to stop running in the hamster wheel without ever truly improving my life or business.

I would spend the next two years slowly recovering, moving from wheelchair to walker to cane to a bad limp. Finally, after several more surgeries, I was back to 90 percent of what I was before the accident. I'll take the A minus, and I will always be incredibly grateful for the recovery and the opportunity to change my life.

THE SAME = MORE OF THE SAME

The truth is you can't move out of "zero to one" mode without true change. You can't simply keep going as you are and expect to somehow scale your business, all while doing less.

You have to take the steps, and sometimes the steps are big steps to take.

As I was rebuilding my body and my life, I realized how drastic some of my own changes needed to be. I disconnected from a lot of people. I put my house on the market. And I restructured my entire business.

Before this point, I always had a "lead from the front" approach. I was the first guy on the jobsite. No one worked harder than me. I was also the one doing the work and often doing the harder work. If one person needed to drive the Bobcat and one needed to shovel concrete, I'd put my guy on the Bobcat and do the shoveling myself.

Again, this mentality worked—to a certain point.

But as soon as I was forced to look at things from a new perspective, I realized just how much I was holding the business back.

As the weeks went on, I realized the business wasn't going to crash. I had hired capable people. I had built enough systems to keep things going. But I was not personally doing the highest-level work or adding the most value I could. I was working in startup mode, still using the initial skills I brought to the work, and therefore my business was capped. I was literally holding my business back.

Does any of this resonate?

If you're honest, do you ever feel like you're running alongside your business, just trying to keep up even though you're exhausted?

If so, you're not alone. As entrepreneurs, we all hit this point. It's what we do when we get there that matters.

A BETTER WAY FORWARD

This book is a guide to turning your business into a cash flow machine, all while you do less. By following the lessons I share, you'll learn how to make money with your mind instead of your time. You'll escape The Hustle Trap. And this will, quite literally, change your life.

Now, don't get me wrong. This will take work. This book is not for someone with a tech startup whose main goal is to raise venture capital. Most of what I share would be useless for this person. That is not the "entrepreneur" I'm speaking to.

This book is for you if you've put in the work, and now you're ready to take things to the next level. You just aren't sure what the next level looks like or how to get there. Maybe you've been at this for years, or maybe you started your business recently. Either way, if you're motivated to go from "zero to one" to "one to two," you're in the right place.

Throughout the book, I will focus on principles and clear take-aways. In each chapter, I'll offer stories and examples that will illustrate how these principles play out.

I focus on principles rather than tools because tools are constantly changing. If I gave you a book full of tools, it would be outdated in a year or two. Principles, on the other hand, last the test of time.

Sometimes it takes a radical event to change your life. I almost had to lose my life to wake up and see where I was holding myself and my business back. But you just shouldn't have to get run over by a truck before you can realize your dreams. If you continually revisit the lessons shared throughout this book, you can transform your business and thereby transform your life.

If all of this sounds great, you might still have one important question: *Why listen to me?*

In short, what I have to offer is experience—the in-the-trenches, learn-by-doing kind of experience. I've been on this entrepreneurial journey for over twenty years now, and I've done it all—excavation, trucking, junk removal, demolition, e-commerce, blockchain, recycling, angel investing, and drafting. Heck, I even started a limo bus company at one point. When my life shifted in 2007, and I began to implement real change in my life and business, I realized just how much time I could have saved kicking myself in the ass.

Today, I run multiple businesses that mostly run themselves—all turning a solid profit each year. I know what truly works and what can be duplicated in any business. When I consult with the CEOs of eight-figure companies or entrepreneurs just getting started, I use the exact principles I share in this book.

I've written this book because I genuinely want to pay it forward. I want to share with you how I actually think and how I replicate success over and over again. All I ask from you is that you let go of your excuses and dive in.

NO EXCUSES

I spend a lot of time with entrepreneurs of all levels. On the surface, these entrepreneurs have nothing in common, but as I dig in, I continually find that they are all crippled by the same affliction: excuses.

Excuses in entrepreneurship are often based on fear of failure or guilt associated with success. Either way, it's easier to create an excuse rather than push forward past the fear.

Take a moment to consider your own excuses. What's holding

you back? Write a list of all of the things that stop you from accomplishing your goals. What makes you believe this is as good as it's going to get or that it's good enough?

Now take a moment to determine that it's time to push past these excuses. Simply making that commitment is the first step. As you read, you'll begin to see how to eliminate each excuse one by one.

As we move into the work, let me leave you with this: life keeps moving, with or without us. And you can come up with every excuse along the way, but those will only hold you back. You have it within you. There's only one question: *Will you take action?*

This is not a book for a select few. It is a book for doers. So, if you're ready to take action, let's dive in!

PART

START WITH YOU

All of the business books in the world can't overcome limiting beliefs.

To escape The Hustle Trap, you have to start with you. So, that's where we'll begin. Now is the time to stop making excuses and take full ownership.

CHAPTER 1

THE RULES HAVE CHANGED

In 1976, the year I was born, my dad started a stationery supplies business. Thirty years later, he sold it. For his time, the business was a great success. It provided him with a good income, freedom to vacation with his family, and ultimately a nice retirement.

He knew that if he put in more time, he could grow the business. But to do that, he'd have to sacrifice time with his family. In his day, he didn't have the tools to multiply himself the way we do today. So, he went to the office every day and managed his company of twelve. He took care of the high-level responsibilities and the day-to-day responsibilities. And he only grew the business to a certain level, never further.

This worked for my dad. He went to work at 5:00 a.m. and was home by 2:00 or 3:00 p.m. most days, and we spent a lot of time vacationing in the mountains—hunting, fishing, boating, and exploring.

Still, even though my dad had it good compared to many, he was always stuck in The Hustle Trap to some degree. In fact, he never would have been able to understand the idea of "escaping The Hustle Trap." For my dad, having a strong work ethic equaled hustling. He learned this from his father, who had owned a construction company. The message passed down was simple: build the thing and then keep it going. In short, *It's all up to you.*

For my father and grandfather, the idea of escaping The Hustle Trap would have made no sense. They were business owners, and that was that. Input equaled output. The more they hustled, the more they made.

Of course, my father and his father before him were only doing what was natural to them; they were doing what they thought was best. But what their generations passed down simply doesn't make sense for our world today.

A NEW WORLD

Past generations of business owners had a formula for success that worked for them. They went to college or an apprenticeship, got a job, worked their way up the ladder until they could own their own business, and then worked in their own business for 30-40 years until they retired (or died). The "hustle your way to success" mindset made sense for them, which is why many Boomers today look down on the younger generations, calling them lazy and entitled.

In reality, most millennials and Gen Zers have simply reprioritized their time. New technologies and globalization have changed the landscape of business, and younger generations know they can leverage this to reclaim their time. Jobs have turned into gigs, and hobbies have turned into side hustles. And some of these gigs and side hustles turn into 6- and 7-figure passive incomes.

Younger generations have figured out the digital equivalent of cloning themselves. Software systems that once cost millions in development and were guarded closely inside of corporate walled gardens are now democratized for the rest of us. Client management software, e-commerce websites, analytics services, and marketing platforms that would have once cost a fortune to build from the ground up are readily available to us all. Just think of platforms like Salesforce, Shopify, Google Analytics, Klayvio, and Hubspot, to name a few. We can use the same software as the big guys for a fraction of what they once cost.

But the changes go beyond technology. Today, a business owner can leverage people in a whole new way. In the past, if a company wanted to outsource to a cheaper labor market, they would have to fly to that country and set up an office, layer in management, and deal with all of the other legalities that came with doing business overseas. Thanks to sites like Fiverr, Upwork, and Draftlancer, you can build a team of highly qualified, motivated freelancers in minutes from your laptop.

It's important to note that these tools and processes work across all industries and not just online businesses. This new world is not only for tech companies. I began leveraging all of these tools in my construction company way back in 2008.

So, no matter what kind of business you are in, new opportunities are at your fingertips. When you optimize these opportunities, you can multiply yourself by 100 and set yourself up for true independence and freedom.

SO WHY DON'T WE CHANGE?

What's interesting about this new world is that many of us still choose to live as if nothing has changed. I know this from firsthand experience. For years, I had a difficult time shifting my approach to business. I ran my demolition company much like my dad did; I kept it small and contained.

Sure, I'd get more work for the crew, but I never learned to leverage people or technology to free myself. My business was capped, and in turn, I was stuck.

There were two reasons I stayed stuck. First, I didn't practice the principles I'm outlining for you in this book. Second, I simply wasn't able to fathom the concept of making more money with less time. That idea didn't compute for me, as it hadn't for my father.

In fact, for a long time, I didn't feel it was even *okay* to work less. It didn't matter how productive or unproductive I was; I simply needed to keep working.

After my life-threatening event in 2007, I was forced to change. I had to find ways to leverage people and technology, and in the process, I realized I could make a lot more without actually doing the work myself. Fast forward to today, when I can easily make 5 or 6 figures per month while hardly doing any work at all.

Recently when I tried to explain to my dad how my businesses run, he didn't get it. None of it made sense to him. Perhaps more telling, none of it felt *right* to him. How can I make in a week what some people work 40-hour weeks to make in a year without doing much, if any, work? How is that okay?

Don't get me wrong. I get where my dad is coming from. I used to feel that guilt too. I don't anymore. And I'm here to tell you that you shouldn't either.

Sure, for argument's sake, let's say there was a time that it would have made sense to equate work ethic and running a business to constant hustling. (In truth, I don't know if my dad or other entrepreneurs of his time were actually capped or if they were simply capped mentally, but I get it; they didn't have what we have today.)

But even if we agree to that, there is absolutely no excuse today. If you're an entrepreneur, there's no reason to simply keep working at the same level for your whole life. And there's certainly no reason to feel guilty if you find ways to work less. If you can create a cash flow machine that works without you, why not? Isn't that what a smart entrepreneur would do?

A WAY OUT OF HUSTLE CULTURE

Here's the hard truth about hustle culture: *it's perpetuated because people can't let it go.*

In many ways, people who feel they simply must keep hustling are like religious zealots. They've sacrificed so much. And when someone's made great sacrifices for something, they cling to it. It can't be wrong. *Hustle, hustle, and keep hustling* can't be wrong!

I certainly clung to that idea until I couldn't anymore.

The first time I truly shifted the way I ran my business, I was still recovering from all of my injuries. I had made the slow progression from walker to crutches to cane to bad limp, but I still couldn't be out there in the field with my guys. I knew they were keeping things running, but I couldn't sit idly by. I wanted to do something to improve the business.

It was in this state that I decided to hire someone from a digital advertising company to run a Google Adwords campaign. I gave him fifty jobs my trucking and demolition company could possibly do, and I told him to let me know what services rose to the top. Within a few days, it was clear: *swimming pool removal* was the winner. The result made sense, given the recession we were in, but I could never have guessed it. This simple use of technology allowed me to dramatically shift my business and focus where there was money.

From there, I decided to build out an iPad app to simplify the bidding process. At the time, this was completely novel for a business like ours, and it proved to pay off big time. I would work with customers on the spot, choosing all the right options for the job—different types of removal (partial engineered, full engineered, and more), size of the pool, and a few other essentials. After I filled out all of the information, I would hit send, and it would go to my staff in Bolivia.

I would tell customers I'd work up the bid in the evening and send it to them. In truth, once I hit send, I never looked at it again. My staff would create the bid and then program the email to send out at 7:00 p.m. This gave the impression that I was putting a lot of work into each quote, but I knew exactly what to charge as soon as I saw the pool. Since the jobs were systematized, highly profitable, and we were doing high volume in no time, I didn't need the bids to be exact.

Most contractors spend hours putting these types of bids together, but my process took a total of about one minute. With just a little upfront work, leveraging the right tools and people, the entire upfront process was automated!

When I first started doing pool removal, we did a pool or two a month. Each brought in $5,000-$10,000 in profit, so I was feeling great. Three months in, I knew it was time to hire another crew and expand. Why not? Everything was systematized. The demand was there. The only thing stopping me from growing was more people. And unlike the old me, I no longer saw a reason to cap myself at a certain number of employees. If another crew equaled a bigger business, it was time for another crew.

Ultimately, there came a point where I had to decide if I wanted to keep putting in the effort on my end to continue growing or if I wanted to create a system that would handle even that part of the equation. I decided to do the latter and found that was where the magic was.

The money started flowing more than it ever had before, but in a way, it wasn't even about the money. It wasn't about a certain dollar amount. What mattered was that everything was flowing, with or without me, with or without my hustling.

And why would I go back?

Since that point, I have built out each of my businesses in the same way. And I'm going to show you how you can do the same in this book.

And believe me, the example I've shared here is not unique to me. Any business owner can leverage technology, people, and systems. This is a repeatable process. But first, you have to change your mindset.

START WITH MINDSET

Reflecting on the past is a useful tool. By looking back, we can realize what we want to change moving forward. Sure, The Hustle Trap may have been the norm in the past. It may have been the norm for you up to this point. But now it's time to shift.

To do this, you must start with your mindset. Everything, in fact, starts with how we think. If you think you must trade time for money, you will. If you believe you can make more and work less, you will find a way. Thankfully, you have this book to help expedite the process, but the process will never even begin without the right mindset.

Some refer to this process as a shift from a "scarcity mindset" to an "abundance mindset." Call it what you want. What matters most to me is getting you from 1 to 2 in your business without all the fear that often accompanies that step. The fear makes sense if scaling means you have to do even more until you run out of steam. But the fear doesn't make sense if scaling means the exact opposite: that you get to do less, much less, while you make more and more.

Here's the good news: if you're willing to change your mindset, your entire life can change. I am a perfect example of this truth. I now live a carefree life. I work when I want. My wife works when she wants. We homeschool because we want our kids to have a flexible schedule. We travel often. I have enough money in the bank that I could live the next thirty years without working if I had to.

I'm not sharing this to boast. I don't spend lavishly or have a bunch of yachts. In fact, I see my greatest purpose in life as providing a means of income for other people. And I'm able to do that because I keep building my businesses the smart way, not the hard way.

Now, before we get ahead of ourselves, I want to be very clear about one thing: there is real work involved here. As we'll see in the next chapter, there's no magic pill. You have to put in the upfront work. I call this frontloading. Creating systems and leveraging tools and people takes time and hard work. But once you take these steps, following what I share throughout this book, you'll be able to look at your business as an outsider, admiring the hard work you've done and enjoying the lifestyle you crave.

So, before we go any further, take a moment to consider where your mindset is. *How does it need to shift? Do you believe that the only way to scale your business is to keep hustling, or do you believe there's a better way?*

I'll let you in on a little secret here: if you don't change your mindset now, you will find yourself in a perpetual state of busyness without pushing yourself and your business forward. So take some time to examine why you think the way you do. Perhaps it's because of messages passed down to you from a different time. Perhaps you know there's a better way, but you're limiting yourself. Either way, it's time for a change.

The other side is fully within grasp *if* you're ready to take ownership. *If* you're ready to be brutally honest with yourself and see where you've capped yourself and your business.

In the next chapters, you'll be challenged to keep uncovering the mental blocks that hold you back so you can move through them.

Don't skip these chapters. Remember: it all starts with mindset. If you don't get this part right, the rest will not flow.

CHAPTER 2

THERE'S NO MAGIC PILL

A year after my near-death experience, my demolition company looked completely different than it had a year before. We now did pool removals almost exclusively. Who could have guessed? Plus, almost everything was now systematized and ran with or without my involvement. There was one major weak point: the operations manager. The person I had in the role was not the right fit, and I knew it.

Instead of blaming the person, I looked at myself. Where could I take ownership of this problem?

The truth was that I hadn't actually put in the upfront work for this role. I didn't know what it required, so I couldn't know who the best person for the job would be. While I knew I wanted to ultimately free myself to work on the business how and when I wanted, I couldn't skip a critical step: doing the work myself. I needed to know this role inside and out.

For two months, I fulfilled all of the duties of the operations manager, noting everything I did so I could share the knowledge with the person I'd hire. After the two months were up, it was time to pass on the role to the right person. Thankfully, I knew exactly who to call.

I met John when he used to sell MRI machines. He had contracted my team to demolish one of the machines, and I got to know the kind of person he was. Now that he was no longer doing that line of work, I called him up. At first, he was hesitant. After all, he'd never been an operations manager for a demolition company. I reassured him that I could teach him everything he needed to learn. And that's exactly what I did.

Over the course of a few weeks, I passed the baton to John, getting him set with all of the essentials. He would, of course, still learn a lot in the role, but I knew he now had what he needed to take full ownership.

After this point, so much shifted in my life. I hadn't realized just how important that role was and what we were missing. The experience taught me an important lesson:

If something isn't working in the business, go back and do the work yourself. Hustle for a while so that you don't have to keep hustling.

In short, I learned that there is never a magic pill to starting and growing a business upfront. There is real work that needs to be done. There's no way around it.

PUT IN THE WORK

So many new entrepreneurs try to find that magic pill. They're looking for someone or something to launch the business into the ether.

Recently, a friend of mine shared with me that he was struggling to grow his clothing company. "I just haven't found the answer," he kept saying. He listed off several potential "answers" he hadn't tried yet: a social media manager, an interview with the CEO of another clothing brand, and raising a bunch of money.

After he explained his position, I looked him straight in the eyes and said, "Tod, there's no answer out there. The answer is you. You've gotta go pound on doors yourself and take the time to learn what your business is and what your customers need. Then, and only then, can you mentor someone to do what you do."

Tod took my words to heart. Some new business owners don't. They simply don't want to hear the hard truth. They ask me for an easier way, and I say there is no easier way. They don't like that, but I'm not sure what else to tell them.

In each business I've had, I've had to put in the work too. This is simply how the world works. It's like a rule of nature.

I remember when I first launched the swimming pool removal service. I had to learn everything, and I mean everything. The end result was truly amazing ($5,000+ profit per removal!), but I didn't get there with a snap of a finger. In fact, it took me fifty bids before I learned how to land one. Along the way, I learned what the customer needed and built an iPad app to streamline the whole bidding process. But the work didn't end there.

Once we finally landed a job, I had to go down to the building department for a permit and learn to draw site plans (the upfront work here allowed me to later create a whole new business). And then it was down to the nitty-gritty learning—figuring out how to climb an excavator into the pool, break tons of gunite, cut through rebar, and compact soil efficiently. I coordinated all of the moving parts of dump trucks moving soil to the site, Bobcats moving soil on the site, compaction with rollers, and grading. I hired a Geotechnical Soils Engineer and learned to work with laborers, building inspectors, and worried homeowners.

You get the point. I had no magic pill. I did the work.

This principle of frontloading holds true no matter what kind of business you're running. But here's the thing: you might have to take three or six months to do the hard work. But if you're willing to invest your energy (and many entrepreneurs aren't), you won't have to tell yourself the same story about why your business isn't working. You'll be free from lying to yourself and free from all the hard work required too.

STOP LOOKING FOR A SAVIOR

"Saviors" come in many forms. A lot of entrepreneurs think they will find a savior in the perfect hire. And sure, a good hire goes a long way. We'll talk more about this in Part 2. But the truth is that no one is going to care about your business as much as you.

Had I relied on a recruiting company to find me an operations manager without doing the work myself, I would have been back in the same place with a bunch of issues on my hands.

Had Tod found the top sales rep in his area, the sales rep would only be able to do so much without Tod first learning how to sell his product.

Another "savior" people look to is money. Too many entrepreneurs today let Silicon Valley define entrepreneurship. Of course, Silicon Valley praises the few companies that raise loads of venture capital.

But raising money doesn't make a business. Money is not the answer. In fact, plenty of startups raise tons of venture capital by selling a dream, and then they fail because they didn't spend time actually building the business. A few years ago, I came across a company that created a juice press machine. All the investors were convinced it would work since the founders equated the machine to a Keurig. Unfortunately, they spent so much of their time raising money that they didn't have a solid product that people would actually buy and use. The company failed, and all of the investors lost their money.

Simple lesson: create a product people actually want to buy and not one that just sounds sexy to investors. It's not about raising money; it's about creating value.

I could go on and on with examples. Year after year, we see multibillion-dollar "unicorns" that turn out to be a sham. Year after year, we see businesses that crash and burn when the economy falters. They're left with nothing because they have no foundation.

Sure, there are many businesses that have successfully raised money and withstood the test of time (such as Paypal and

Amazon), but the difference is that these businesses actually had a strong foundation. A good business owner knows that the foundation is everything; *if you have a strong foundation, you can always rebuild.*

If you find yourself spending 90 percent of your time looking for funds (or any other savior) and only 10 percent of your time building the business, stop!

Stop looking for a savior and start doing the work.

START FROM THE BOTTOM

In order to be an entrepreneur, you need a builder's mentality. You need to build that strong foundation. The parts underground are far more important than what's above ground. But everything is reliant on that foundation.

If you haven't done the upfront work, go back. If you find a part of your business that is lacking—and causing you endless stress—go back. Start from the bottom, and build from there.

Even the idea of going back and starting from the bottom might feel demoralizing, especially if you've been working on your business for years. But you'll be surprised about the effect working from the bottom will have on your business. It will, ultimately, free you from The Hustle Trap.

CHAPTER 3

STOP MAKING EXCUSES

Excuses are the avoidance of pain. Pain equals growth. Therefore, excuses stunt growth.

In some of my off-time, I like to mentor guys at halfway houses. Many of them have been in prison for a long time, and now they're trying to get their lives together. I've found one of the best ways I can help them is to show them how they are making excuses. This realization actually liberates them to move forward and start something of their own.

I remember mentoring one guy who told me how he took great pride in cleaning kitchens in the prison. He was always praised by the inspector, and once he got out he knew he wanted to start a cleaning business. I said, "Great, so what are you doing?"

He went on to explain that he wanted to raise $50,000 because he needed to hire someone, needed a truck, and needed cleaning supplies. Needed all kinds of things.

After he went on for a while, I stopped him and said, "Why do you need all of that?"

He looked at me confused, so I explained: "You can go down the street and knock on doors to restaurants and get your first customer. What is the minimum amount of things you need to do that?"

After some back and forth, he realized he had almost everything he needed already. He simply needed to start. Sure, there would be a time when he would start bringing in enough that he could hire and mentor someone else, then get more equipment and all the rest, but right now, he didn't need any of that. He simply needed to stop making excuses.

One of the other guys in the program wanted to start a construction company and knew he'd need to first find a job at one to gain experience. But there was just one problem (in his mind): he didn't have a driver's license. In my first meeting with him, I helped him get over the excuse by scheduling an appointment to get his permit. After he went and got it, he texted me: *Holy shit, I actually got my permit.* This was a major moment for him, and it wasn't at all as far off as he had imagined.

Many of the guys love my approach, not because I have something mind-blowing to share, but simply because I'm getting them past their excuses so they can move forward. Many of the other volunteers work in Venture and Tech and simply can't understand where these guys are coming from or the idea of working from the bottom. When they hear a different way, beyond excuses, something clicks.

Of course, it's not only ex-cons who make excuses. In fact, on the other side of the spectrum, millionaires often have many more excuses and don't want to hear the hard truth. They are more hard-headed than the guys in halfway houses who are willing to try anything.

For a while, I consulted with a millionaire who was overwhelmed by his business and wanted to sell it. He saw no other way. So, I asked him what would need to happen to fix the business. As we investigated, we realized there were people issues and systems issues. I knew these could turn into his biggest assets, so I decided to help him clean things up. "At the least," I said, "you can make your business more appealing to a buyer."

In this case, the business owner faced some true obstacles, but what he couldn't see was how to stop making excuses so that he could get over those obstacles. For example, one of his salespeople was completely unmotivated. That was an obstacle. The excuse, though, was that he couldn't fire this person and find someone who wanted to be in the role. Once he did, his sales organization shifted. All in all, the changes he needed to make in the people arena took less than a month. Then, for the next three months, we worked on systems issues.

After month four, I checked in and asked if he was ready to sell. "No way," he said. "Things are running better than they ever have." He suddenly had more free time, more cash flow, and the ability to pursue more of the things he loves in his life. There was no longer a reason to sell.

Again, this business owner faced real issues, but that didn't mean he was off the hook. He was saying he couldn't handle the business, but what he really meant was that he couldn't handle it in the state it was and that he wasn't willing to fix the problems.

No matter where you are in your business, you absolutely must locate the excuses, so you can stop making them.

OBSTACLES VERSUS EXCUSES

In many cases, you, too, will come up against real obstacles. But you have the choice to keep complaining about it or find a way to overcome those obstacles.

When I first started my hauling company in college, I had only one old truck. It broke down often, and I wished I could get a new truck so that we'd have more uptime.

There was just one problem: I didn't think I could actually qualify for a loan for a new truck. But the truth was, I didn't know if this was an excuse or a true obstacle. When I went down to get the loan, I found out that I actually did have an obstacle. I was new in business and had little credit built up. By checking, however, I found out that I wasn't far off from what I needed. Sure enough, I put in the work, built my credit, and a year later I was able to buy two new trucks.

In many cases, we think people are the obstacles in our businesses, and maybe they are. But the excuse is that we can't do anything about it. Early in my demolition company, I hired someone who had extreme anger issues. He was horrible to the customers, but I was convinced I had to keep him because he could drive a tractor, and I didn't think I could find a replacement. In truth, I hadn't put in the effort to find a replacement.

Within a couple of months of him coming on, he quit. So, what then? I was forced to go out and drive the tractor myself until I could find someone new. And sure enough, I found someone with a great attitude who could do the task. In short, I was forced to overcome the obstacle and get over my excuse.

Today, I often use the "What if?" question to help people see where they have excuses rather than true obstacles. When I talk to people who are sick of their jobs and want to leave them to start a business, I ask, "What if you went in to work tomorrow and there was a pink slip on your desk?" After all, that could happen, right? It happens all the time. This simple question helps the person realize they don't actually have an obstacle; they have an excuse. They are leaving their future in the hands of others rather than taking it into their own hands.

One thing to realize about obstacles is that they are not an end in themselves. Even if you are facing a true obstacle, it's actually there to point you in the direction you need to go. You have to get around it one way or another, so you might as well start finding a way now.

A GOOD ENOUGH STORY CAN FOOL YOU

One of the other ways entrepreneurs make excuses is by telling stories—to themselves and to others.

When I moved to LA, I realized everyone was great at story-telling. Some of these stories even got me. I invested in several companies because I was fooled by the story when I should have dug deeper to discover the gaps.

I've been through enough of these stories now to know they all sound the same: too good to be true. They are so well crafted because the person has repeated them so many times over the years. Now, I've learned to listen very carefully. If a story is too well crafted, there are reasons to question it.

On the other hand, I know when someone is truly trying to figure out the problem. I respond much differently if someone says, "I've been doing X religiously every week for nine months, and I just can't seem to crack this. I want it so badly, but I don't know how to get there." This person isn't making excuses; they simply need some direction.

The point is this: *each of us needs to know where we are truly facing obstacles versus telling stories and fooling ourselves.*

TEST YOURSELF

In the end, you need to question yourself. Are you simply telling stories without a real business behind you? Do you know you can't actually fulfill the promises you're making? If your answer is yes to either of those questions, it may be time to fold and walk away. You may not be the right person to run the business. Or it may simply not be the right time for it.

I have had many friends who have been unwilling to see where they are lying to themselves. Years ago, one of my friends started raising money for a company similar to Uber. The only problem was that he had no tech chops and didn't know the transportation industry. So, he started building a company in the vision of his dream, not a company for his customer. Guess what? To this day, he is still raising money and simply can't look at the truth: that the business is not going to work.

At some point, these situations turn into fraud. I had a friend whose business had a huge ramp-up because of some notoriety in the media, but afterward, everything started going downhill. The business simply wasn't going to work, but he kept telling the same story. To this day, he's still taking orders, even though manufacturing has completely halted. He claims he will one day fulfill these orders, but it's hard to believe he can. He is one of the nicest people I know, but he simply can't face the reality of the sunk cost. He keeps telling the same story to appease investors when what he really needs to do is let go.

I share these stories because they are the epitome of excuses. You don't overcome excuses simply by belief or thinking something "can't fail." You overcome excuses by looking at things honestly and then putting in the work. And in some cases, the hard work is to walk away. This might seem like a strange piece of advice in a book about growing your business, but I share it so that you don't find yourself stuck in a place you don't want to be years down the road. Failure, regardless of cost, is an education, and it's a part of the process of becoming an entrepreneur.

Look at everything honestly. Test yourself. Where are you making excuses? Where are you telling yourself or others stories?

If you're making an excuse, it's time to make a change, one way or another. Once you're willing to address the excuse, then and only then can you move on in your business (or another altogether).

CHAPTER 4

IT'S YOUR FAULT (EVEN IF IT'S NOT)

After I graduated from high school, I was one of the only kids in my school not going to college. I took a lot of flak for this, but I knew traditional school just wasn't right for me at the time. I wanted to learn. I wanted to expand my mind. But I wasn't finding what I was looking for in school.

After graduating, I read a lot and remember coming across texts by William Edwards Deming, who was a statistician who helped with the census and economy in Japan after World War II. While Deming was in Japan, he discovered the idea of Kaizen or *continual improvement over time*. Deming looked at improvement as a constant and ongoing process.

This idea resonated with me. I always wanted to improve, and when I later found myself with a new business, I wanted to improve that too.

While I was coming from a good place, I couldn't see how I was missing the bigger picture of improvement. When things simply didn't get better in the business, I grew extremely frustrated. I remember coming home to my girlfriend and complaining about all of the things my guys were doing wrong. "Another truck got loose and hit a house." "Someone else is stealing money from the recycling business." One time, I even had to pull over on the side of the freeway just to yell at the top of my lungs. I felt out of control.

This continued until another business owner asked me a simple question: "How can you own that?"

The question stopped me in my tracks and shifted my perspective. Instead of spending my time feeling frustrated or blaming others, I could ask myself what I had not yet done *and* what I could do to fix the issues.

The first step was to acknowledge that I had hired these people in the first place. If they weren't the right fit, I needed to be the one to make a change.

I also needed to get practical. *What could I do for the issue of the runaway truck?* The guys would use a chock block if they had one. The problem was they constantly forgot them, leaving them on jobsites all over the place. So, I decided to weld a chain from the truck to the chock block. In addition, I added a walk-around policy for anytime a truck was moved. Sure enough, the issue was fixed in no time. No more trucks rolling off.

What could I do for the issue in the recycling business? I could first acknowledge that if most people have the opportunity to steal, they will. I could then acknowledge that my accounting systems were mediocre at best. If I wanted people to stop people from stealing, I needed to fix these systems. And what I could do immediately was stop using cash. So I did.

Little by little, all my complaints turned into to-do lists that would fix the problems. Little by little, the blaming turned into choices I could make.

YOU'RE THE CAPTAIN, SO ACT LIKE IT

Imagine being a captain on a ferry. While looking over the side, you slip and fall into the water. If you find yourself sinking, are you thinking about who spilled their drink that you slipped on or why the railing wasn't higher? NO! You are thinking of how to swim back to the boat and how to get back on board.

Fault doesn't matter; solutions matter.

When you climb back on board, you think about how this could have happened to a small child or elderly person. If you are a good captain, your full effort will go to how you will not let this happen again. You don't try to track down the person who spilled the soda or pull out the blueprints to find out who made the rails so low. You print signs that state "No Drinking or Eating on the Boat." You hire a welder to add railings along the side of the boat. *You* make the changes.

Take a moment to consider where you get frustrated in your own business. Where does the energy from that frustration go? If it goes toward the employee for doing something wrong, you might win temporarily. That employee might never make that same mistake again. But you don't win long-term. Someone else will come along and make the same mistake unless you create a system to ensure it never happens again. Mistakes made by employees, vendors, and contractors are opportunities to improve your business. If you do nothing to ensure they don't happen, it's your fault. Simple as that.

FREE YOURSELF

When I first made this shift in my business and took full owner-ship of everything, I realized I had a whole new sense of control. I was no longer beholden to whatever might happen because "I can't do anything about it." Instead, I was liberated to see the problems and make changes.

In the end, this new way of thinking led to hundreds of systems in my business that keep things running smoothly. Of course, I know issues will still arise, even with these systems in place. What's different now is that my mindset for continual improve-ment leads me to keep making necessary changes rather than becoming frustrated that everything isn't already perfect.

In my consulting work, one of the main problems I see among business owners is that they are completely stuck in the blame game. Blaming their employees. Blaming the government. Blaming the regulatory system. As soon as they release the blame, they walk around with a whole new sense of freedom, no longer stuck in a cycle that never ends.

Release the blame. Take the ownership. It will free you.

PRACTICE BY JOURNALING

One of the best ways to notice where you're stuck in blame and need to take ownership is through journaling. You can start by running through different areas where you keep making the same complaints. Then ask, *How can I own that?*

When you find yourself frustrated by something in your business, write it down. Here's an example of how to move through the process so an answer can surface:

1. What happened?

We had a jobsite shut down by the city because a truck tracked mud down the road and was then tracked by other cars, which made a huge mess.

2. Who was involved?

My truck driver. He knew that tracking dirt down the road is illegal and would likely cause a jobsite shutdown. Yet, he forgot.

3. What was my role?

I had failed to set up a system ensuring truck tires were washed prior to leaving the jobsite. There was an unexpected rain that turned what would have been a little dust into a muddy mess, and because I didn't have a system in place, no one did anything different than usual.

4. What can I do to make sure it doesn't happen again?

Create a double gating system when a truck pulls off of a jobsite where they are driving on dirt. When they pass through the first gate, they pull onto a concrete surface, exit their truck, and close the gate behind them. On the gate in front of them, it says, "Do not open this gate until you walk around your truck and ensure the following: *Tires are free from mud and debris *Dump body ledges are free from rocks or debris that can fall off *Truck is properly tarped to contain load *Windshield is clean with full visibility. There is a pressure washer, broom, and window squeegee next to the truck. Once the truck is prepped, the driver snaps a picture and sends it to the office with the message "Truck prepped, en route to dumpsite."

You might notice in this example how specific I was about the solution. This is important; be specific! Again, this is all about ownership. Don't half-ass it. This business is yours. The effort you put into it will ultimately determine how well it runs and how quickly you can create a cash flow machine that makes money for you.

CHAPTER 5

KNOW WHO'S ON BOARD

When you are getting your business off the ground, you often make decisions to preserve capital, rapidly onboard customers, and cut costs. You'll also hire anyone who's willing to put up with the non-stop demands of a new business. These early decisions might help your company take off, but they can also cripple your business as you continue to grow.

Once your business is off to the races, you need to re-evaluate every part of your business to make sure that these things that helped create early success don't stand in your way in getting to the next level.

This is especially true when it comes to the people in the business.

When I started my first business, Hauling Pros, I started with a business partner, Matt, who did the fieldwork while I was in my college classes. Once we got off the ground, I realized that my partner had a very different idea of how to run a business.

He was focused on short-term revenue. He would often flake on smaller jobs to take on higher-priced ones. While I appreciated his hunger to bring in more money each week, I cared much more about long-term growth. I knew that a $99 customer might hire us once a week, while the $400 job might only be a one-time gig.

Additionally, Matt wanted to charge as much as possible whenever he could, whereas I wanted to have set pricing we'd tell customers over the phone. The set pricing meant we only needed to go to the jobsite once rather than going once to provide a quote and once to do the work. It also allowed us to hold our prices in winter, when all the other companies discounted their services because it was a slower time for business.

Eventually, I decided the differences between Matt and me were simply too great. He was a friend and also ex-military like me. He was one of the hardest-working guys I knew. I had nothing against him, but the business partnership simply wasn't going to work long-term.

I sat down with him and told him that I was grateful for what we had built, but I thought it was best if we parted ways. I then proposed a buyout. I would pay him $6K and give him one of our trucks, or he could pay me $6K and let me take one of the trucks. Either way, I wanted to separate amicably. He took the deal. I later found out that he took the money to rent a limo bus and party with his friends in San Francisco and blew it all.

Had I kept trying to make things work with Matt, it would have become even more complicated and more expensive to go our separate ways. By making the choice to separate, I was able to structure the business in a way that was primed for long-term growth and profitability. The next year, the landfill told me our trucks were arriving ten times as much as any competitor, and the business kept growing—tripling three years in a row.

Later down the line, I had a similar situation occur when I hired Shawn, a guy I knew back in college. Remember the gap in my business that I referenced before? This was Shawn. I brought him on as an "operations manager," when in truth, he was managing the phone while I was working on-site with the crew. Over time, he became a real drain on my business. Not only was I paying him way too much, but he had a complete disregard for the business. He started hiding things from me, and I caught him in his lies.

Finally, after ten years, I had taken so much responsibility away from him (so that he couldn't mess things up any further) that he quit.

This was when I took time to figure out what I really needed. I learned the ins and outs of the operations manager role, hired the right person for the job, and also brought on an office lady to manage the phones. Now my business was finally running how it should have all along.

THE DESIGNER AND THE ENGINEER

Many companies are founded by two friends with similar back-grounds. Often these friends are both marketers (designers) or both operations (engineers), but to have a well-balanced business, you need both beauty and function. You don't want a beautiful building that will collapse a couple of months in.

You also don't want an ugly concrete block simply because it will stand forever.

Take, for example, the classic story of two marketers who decided to start their own business. They build a beautiful site and the best funnels. They might even manage to get some customers through those funnels and make their first sales. The only problem is that they have no operations chops. They don't think like engineers. They both think like designers. So, in no time, they have a two-star rating on Yelp, and their business is slowly headed to its death.

On the opposite end of the spectrum, some businesses start with two engineers who don't consider design at all. This was the case with a stroller company, which failed because two engineers (two men, by the way) decided to build the most structurally sound stroller in the world. Unfortunately, the stroller was enormous and difficult to handle. Sure, it wouldn't break, but does that matter if a mother can't even use it to take her baby on a walk?

Consider your own situation. If you started your business with a friend, it's likely you shared a lot in common. This isn't necessarily a bad thing, but in business, you need balance. It might be time to reevaluate what you're missing. Who are you, and who are others in the business? What are your strengths and weaknesses? And where do you need to fill the gaps?

MAKE STRUCTURAL CHANGES

I'm part of a CEO support group, and one of the main points of conversation in the group is business partners. Many of the issues that arise in business are because the person who founded it is unwilling to look honestly at what's working and what is not when it comes to that partnership.

The truth is that many partnerships start for moral support but don't work out in the long run. Again, you have to be willing to review. Is it still working? What structural changes need to be made?

This process takes time, and a big part of it is learning who you are and what you bring. I've learned, for example, that I work most like a Chief Marketing Officer and big-picture CEO, and I now know who I need as a partner or partners. In my business, Dirt Match, I work with a partner who functions as a Chief Operations Manager and another who functions as a Chief Technology Officer. Together, we each fill in what the others don't have.

Remember our goal here. I want to get you past zero to one and help you shift into second gear and beyond. Zero to one is sloppy. It's a lot of hard work, and it makes sense for you to do that work yourself. But at some point, you can only do so much as one person. If you want to get to the next stage as an entrepreneur, you have to stop all the hustling—doing everything, fixing everything. You need to be able to let go, which requires having the right people on board.

We will talk more about this in Part 2. For now, consider if it's time to bring on the next right person. If you're still responsible for twelve things, making $400,000 a year, it's time to reevaluate. It's time to hire someone at $100,000 a year to take six of the twelve things from you.

Ultimately, the goal is freedom. To reach freedom, you'll need to continually reexamine who you have on board and what changes or additions need to be made.

CHAPTER 6

LIFE IS SHORT, MONEY IS ABUNDANT

I remember graduating from college when my dad, the business owner, asked me how I'd use my college degree to get a job. By this point, I was already making six figures a year and wondered why in the world I would want to go get a job for $40,000 a year. It just didn't make sense.

Even though my dad was an entrepreneur, he wanted the best for me and always advocated for the "safe" route forward. To him, the safe route was the "American dream" of getting a good job, being there for thirty years, and having a pension plan when all was said and done. I was thinking in the exact opposite way.

A few years later, after my accident, I read the *4-Hour Work Week* by Tim Ferris. The book helped me imagine how I could automate even more, but it also helped me realize why my father and I thought differently. In short, it takes a certain kind of person to see the value in risk.

Entrepreneurship offers the possibility of living and working on your own terms with the potential of capturing the full value of your output. While it is risky to make the leap into entrepreneurship, once you are successful, you can mitigate that risk.

The truth is that 99 percent of people want security, and entrepreneurs are the ones who offer it to them, leveraging the people-power to multiply themselves and ultimately make a lot more. This doesn't mean entrepreneurs are guaranteed a certain amount of financial success; it simply means they operate differently.

This isn't a good or bad, right or wrong thing. It just is. If you're an entrepreneur willing to take the risk and be strategic, own your place, and let others own theirs.

BAD EMPLOYEES CAN MAKE FOR GREAT ENTREPRENEURS

When I was 19, I moved from the Bay Area to San Diego and bummed around for a while—playing chess at the beach and waiting tables. Eventually, I saw the path was leading nowhere and talked to a military recruiter, who told me I could get money for college if I joined. So, before I knew it, I had a combat arms job and was on my way to Germany. Within a few weeks, I was in my first war zone in Bosnia for a peacekeeping mission. Since I had grown up in a fairly sheltered, middle-class home, I grew up a lot during this time. One way I didn't grow, however, was in compliance. In fact, it was in the military that I realized I would make for a terrible employee.

The inefficiencies, which were either a byproduct of "this is the way we've always done it" or a means to keep soldiers busy, always confounded me. If I tried to create a system to improve efficiency, it was looked on as an attack on the status quo and was quickly shot down by the chain of command. So instead of looking for ways to improve my military experience, I came to laugh at it. I would be told to sweep the motor pool even though I just did it the night before, and there wasn't a speck of dust on the floor. I guess the walls covered in grease didn't matter. No, the protocol was for me to sweep.

Towards the end of my time in the military, I remember my command Sergeant Major telling me I could have a good career in the military and that there wouldn't be anything for me in the outside world. As a response, I told him to look me up when he got out, and I'd give him a job. I knew I couldn't stay long in any job where I simply had to comply; I knew my destiny was to be an entrepreneur. Of course, to get there, I had to be willing to work hard and take risks.

When I got out and went to college, I worked my ass off. I got straight As and found a job at a restaurant. My parents' house burning down two weeks after I got out of the military threw a wrench in things, especially after the insurance for a hotel room ran out, and I found myself sleeping in my old 1983 Honda Accord and on friends' couches.

But rock bottom wasn't going to stop me. In fact, rock bottom seems to be where I've always found my greatest strength— something I share in common with many entrepreneurs.

I've always tried to leverage what I have rather than focus on my challenges. So, I worked hard studying and received an academic scholarship to St. Mary's College of California. I got a job at a local restaurant and moved my way up from waiter to bouncer to bartender and eventually manager. Along with the $1,200 a month tax-free GI bill, I was doing pretty well. But I didn't want to stop there. I was ready to make my next move, so I started Hauling Pros, my first company, while still in college.

It was humble beginnings. At first, I bought a little Chevy and a trailer to hitch to it. I'd drive to construction sites, load it up, and take it to the dump. From there, I got bigger trucks and eventually invested in a dump truck. Soon enough, people were asking if I could do demolition as well. I got all of the necessary licenses for demolition and was off to the races. The trucks got bigger. The equipment got bigger. The crew got bigger.

So, I decided to start a couple of other companies and replicate what I had done. One turned into a good-sized demolition and general engineering company. In another, I owned several recycling centers around the Bay where we recycled electronics, mattresses, and appliances. Another focused on property preservation—we would fix up foreclosures for banks. At one point, I even had a limo bus company, but that was short-lived.

It was all about putting ideas to work and seeing what grew. Sometimes, the growth came from unexpected places. Hauling Pros, for example, became a success because my truck broke down. Since this was my only truck, I couldn't service my customers without it. So, when I got it back up and running, I decided I needed a backup truck and hired a friend who needed a job. Soon, I decided it was time for another truck and time to hire another unemployed friend. By the time I graduated college, I had ten trucks and almost twenty guys working for me, doing more than $1 million a year in business.

After I graduated, I had another epiphany of why I would make for a bad employee. Whenever I would lose motivation, I would find myself traveling until I found it again. When I would come back, I'd be in a flow state where I'd work seven days a week, relentlessly improving my business. A concentrated four weeks in flow state was the equivalent of six months of work in any other state.

Of course, a typical employer would never let me have this schedule, even if I could 10X his business. He would ascribe to me the typical two weeks of vacation and fifty-plus weeks of my butt in the chair, regardless of my motivation.

What I've discovered along the way is that many of the best entrepreneurs weren't necessarily the best employees or the best students, for that matter. There's a reason for the phrase, "The A and B students will work for the C and D students." In the end, it's all about building a life according to your strengths. If you see things differently than most people, that's okay. Use who you are and what you have to your advantage.

AMPLIFY YOURSELF

The wealth in the world is infinite; it's just a matter of tapping into it.

I like to imagine all the wealth in the world is hovering above us, just out of reach. Every now and then, we can find a low point and poke a hole in it. Out comes the profit. But what if we could multiply that? Anyone can spend $1 million and make $1 million (looking at you, startup tech founder), but if you can spend $1 million and make $1.1 million, now you've made some "alpha"—results that are truly above the norm.

Now, what's truly magical is when you learn to amplify yourself. Remember, you're just one person. No matter how smart you are, you can only do so much. But through the right people and systems, now you can cut a hole in the atmosphere and see the money start flowing in a whole new way.

This is what it means to make yourself larger than yourself. The first way to do this is to leverage yourself, and we'll explore how to do exactly that in Part 2.

SCALE THROUGH PEOPLE

You have now looked at yourself honestly. You've evaluated where you are, and you know the changes you need to make. Now it's time to scale. To do this, you need to find the right people and stop trying to do it all on your own. You've had the hustle mindset. Now it's time for a whole new mindset—the efficiency mindset—to kick in. Now it's time to have others hustle for you.

Those in a scarcity mindset often feel that using the labor of others to enrich self is exploitation. I counter this by saying there is no better way to serve society than to offer employment to those willing to work. Hiring one person for $60K per year will have 10X the effects of donating $60K to a social cause. Giving money to a cause might give a meal, but giving employment gives purpose and a meal at the same time.

In the end, remember that business is about people, so don't skimp here.

CHAPTER 7

FIND AMAZING PEOPLE, NOW

My first couple of years in business, I would hire anyone. I just needed a body—someone to fill the role. I had no idea how to hire people. I thought it was just about hiring a body that could drive a truck. Because I hadn't mastered this part of my business, I created a ton of headaches for myself.

Soon enough, I realized I simply wasn't treating the hiring process with respect. Now I think of it this way: you should put the same kind of care into hiring a new employee that you would into hiring a nanny to watch your child. You would never place an ad on Craigslist "looking for anyone available to watch my five-year-old, no references needed."

When I started respecting the hiring process and implementing some new hiring methods, everything shifted. I started, for example, paying my employees $1,000 to help me find the right person. They, of course, were intrinsically motivated. They wanted someone great on the team too. And if they did help bring someone on, they'd hold them accountable. Since they referred them, any poor performance would negatively affect their reputation.

Over the years, I've developed more intricate systems for hiring certain roles. If I put out an advertisement for a new architect, for example, I'll give several tests to evaluate candidates. Out of a hundred candidates, I might pay $20 to the top twenty to take a small test. Then I'll narrow down again and again, paying for tests until I reach a final three. I'll pay each of these three candidates $100 to take one final test and choose the person who really stands out—not only in their work but in who they were as a person. Now that I also know the other two and have vetted them thoroughly, I can bring them on later if needed.

Most importantly, I've realized that hiring the right person requires knowing who they actually are. After qualifying a candidate, I'll always ask more general questions about their lives. Values and personality show up fast in these conversations. If someone starts talking bad about their previous boss or how poorly things were run at their previous job, I know they're not the right person for my business. If they come in and rub me the wrong way, no matter how impressive their resume, I'll pass. On the other hand, if it's easy to talk to someone and they have a positive attitude from the start, I'm much more interested in getting to know them further. These are the kinds of people I want around; they bring energy to everything and everyone, and that's invaluable.

The truth is, amazing people are out there; you just have to find them.

DIFFERENT WAYS TO WIN

Once you do find the right people, it's then time to entrust them with the relevant tasks. This means letting go of control and recognizing the strengths each person brings to the table.

When I was run over by a truck and almost died, I realized the guys on my team were able to keep things going. Not only that, but they ran everything really well. Sure, I noticed that one or two of the twenty guys still needed to be managed closely, but these were the guys I needed to let go of anyway. For the most part, I had simply been projecting the need to look over everything and micromanage.

During this time, I was forced to let go of my ego and recognize that I didn't have to do everything. I didn't have to control everything. In fact, others on the team could do the tasks just as well or better than I.

Some amazing things happen when you learn to let go. One of the most important things I learned was how to truly see someone else's strengths. I finally realized that just because someone had a different approach, it didn't mean that approach wouldn't work.

I learned this firsthand when I hired my first salesperson for my demolition company. Up to that point, I had handled all the sales. I could instill confidence by speaking to my experience and knowledge of the trade with potential customers. Eventually, I knew I needed to hire someone else for the role and brought on someone I immediately connected with. He had a completely different approach and made drinking buddies out of every customer. Still, he closed about 80 percent using his strengths. Had I tried to force him to do things my way, it wouldn't have worked for him.

This was a lesson in letting go and leveraging what someone else had to offer. I realized that success comes in many different forms and that allowing people to grow into their own strengths will always produce better results than forcing them into a role or way of being that goes against their nature. You want to find their unique strengths and nurture those. Of course, you have to set a framework for them, but then let them grow into their own genius.

In some cases, you learn what a person's true zone of genius is over time. Recently, I hired an executive assistant. The woman I hired seemed like a great person, but over time I noticed she simply wasn't cutting it when it came to the actual tasks. I needed her to be proactive in taking notes at every meeting, in going out and researching things on her own, and, in general, being on top of everything, so I didn't have to think about it all. But when I looked closer, the problem wasn't with her. It was that she was in the wrong role.

When we talked, I realized she was a great communicator and decided to transition her to a customer service role. Sure enough, she thrived in this new role. Not only did the customers love her, but she was much happier.

So often, it's not about not being able to find amazing people. It's simply about being able to find where they shine. It's also important to understand that most people have an upper limit when it comes to promoting within your company. Just because someone is an amazing customer service rep doesn't mean they should be promoted to a customer service team manager. Many companies promote people to their highest level of incompetence. When someone is thriving in a position, be careful about how you reward that person. Promotion often isn't the answer. Look at more vacation days, higher pay, or other means of reward first. And if you want to promote from within, be sure to test the candidates just like you would test candidates from outside the company.

BE THE SPECTATOR

In Part 1, we focused on taking ownership and frontloading. That is all necessary. There was a time I needed to be the one swinging the sledgehammer. There was a time you needed to be on the field too. But now we're moving on. We're moving past hustle into a whole new phase of business. And to do that, you have to stop being the player and become the spectator.

You can see the full field from the command post. From here, you entrust the people you've hired and then trust the systems you put in place to alert you when anything is off. We'll talk more about systems in Part 3.

For now, the important step to take is a step back—off the field. This step might hurt the ego a little. Up until now, you've done it all. But think about it: there's no way to give 100 percent to every single role as one person. No, you want one person committed to each role, giving it their all.

So, be the spectator, not the player. Stop stalling and start hiring.

CHAPTER 8

HIRE POTENTIAL

When I was managing the everyday tasks of the general engineering business, I started to get a visitor to the office each week. The man had long hair and was built like an ox, with tattoos all over. What I found most interesting and somewhat humorous, however, was how he always showed up in a suit. This was, after all, a place where everyone wore jeans, dirty shirts, and steel-toed boots.

From the start, the man was upfront with me that he had recently gotten out of prison, but he would do anything for a job. I didn't have a job for him, but I was impressed by his consistency in showing up each week in a suit to ask about openings.

Eventually, he simply wore me down, and I'm glad he did. I recognized in him the same tenacity I had when I was a young man and would do anything to make some money, and once I brought him on, I realized he was ten times more motivated than some of the guys on the crew who were half-assing it. What

I learned from this experience is that for many roles, it can be best to hire potential, not always credentials.

Looking back over my 20+ years as an entrepreneur, my absolute best employees have been with me for the long haul. When they came aboard, they had few skills, but they were hungry for work, and they genuinely cared about doing a good job.

It's important to remember that the hard-working skilled workers will never be out of a job. They will never apply to your employment ad. They either stay with their current company, or they are scouted by another, but they are rarely unemployed.

So when you place an employment ad for skilled workers, you're already playing against the odds. If you instead play the long game and hire motivated, hard-working people and nurture them into skilled workers, you will build a bulletproof staff over time.

FIND THE MOTIVATED ONES

Remember hustle? Well, hustle should be a trait you look for in your employees. You want people who will work relentlessly in their role. The salespeople who pursue clients until the sale is made. The operator who gets one job after another done at record speed. The marketing director who chases after growth like their life depends on it.

When hiring, I always look past the resume. I ask more important questions. *What makes this person wake up every day and come to work? Are they newly married? Do they have a new baby? Did they just move to the area, just scraping by?*

I think like this because I've been this person. I've also been the single guy who parties on the weekends. I worked the absolute hardest when (early in adulthood) I was waking up in the back seat of my car or a friend's couch knowing I deserved a better life and when (later in my life) people I loved relied on me.

To find the motivated ones, you have to find their motivation and then be their solution. Give them a path to a better life. This is not only best for your business, but it is fulfilling too.

And if the time comes and they do decide to move onto a larger company with benefits you can't afford, congratulate them, encourage them, and be happy for them. Their life is better because of *you*. There's nothing more rewarding in life than to recognize and nurture someone's talent and be a part of their growth, with or without your company. I promise your investment in others will come full circle.

So, find the motivated ones, invest in them, build them up, and watch your business flourish.

CHAPTER 9

THE HIDDEN COST OF UNDERSTAFFING

When I ran the demolition company, I made sure to have several people in unskilled labor positions. One might be on a jobsite to sweep things up. Another might run to the store to get a can of oil, so the equipment operator didn't need to do that himself. I might have another hop on a Bobcat to try it out and see if they had a knack for it.

By overstaffing by about 5 or 10 percent consistently, I always had enough people available and was rarely caught in a position where the responsibility fell back on me.

This wasn't always the case. I initially only hired when I absolutely needed someone. In a service-based business, where the biggest expense is labor, it was easy to get caught thinking this was the place to cut costs. But it didn't take long for me to realize how running too lean in this area put me in a difficult position. Many times, I had to actually fill the position myself, and that got old fast.

Moreover, I realized that even good employees can take advantage of a situation if you give them too much leverage. And sure enough, I started having people call out sick often. I'd have others who didn't give it their all some days. They knew they were all I had.

So, when I finally did de-leverage my employees by overstaffing, they no longer had the upper hand. I reclaimed the leverage for myself.

HEALTHY COMPETITION

As I said in the last chapter, nurturing staff from the bottom and bringing them up through your organization is the best way to build long-term, solid employees. Keeping this pipeline open and running even when you don't necessarily have a need for entry-level positions has another benefit. Promoting within your organization keeps everyone in check. When people know that someone is gunning for their position, they show up.

The system works for itself.

The takeaway here is simple: overstaff and promote from within. This way, you will still be able to operate lean while always having enough bandwidth and not being held hostage by your employees. You will, in fact, be constantly nurturing the next rockstar employees that will help take your business to the next level.

CHAPTER 10

SET POSITIVE FEEDBACK LOOPS

In my drafting business, the customer receives the drafted plan from their designer within 24 hours. Along with the plan is a note that reads: *In the next couple of days, you will receive an email asking about the service you received. It would mean a lot to me if you left a 5-star review with a note about your experience. If, for whatever reason, you don't feel you received 5-star service, please let me know what I can do to get you there.*

This way, the customer knows upfront that we want to get them exactly what they need. The designer is also incentivized to make the customer happy, knowing that whenever they get a 5-star review, I'll kick back a nice little bonus to them. This is a positive feedback loop, and it all works on its own. The customer's happy. The designer's happy. I'm happy.

Positive feedback loops help you align your customers, your employees, and your profitability.

To set them up in your business, you'll have to think creatively about ways to effectively support everyone at the same time.

SPOT NEGATIVE FEEDBACK LOOPS TOO

On the flip side, you want to eliminate negative feedback loops as soon as you see them. I had to learn this the hard way several times.

I first learned the lesson in my hauling business. I noticed one of my guys was consistently selling less than all of the others. While the others were selling up to $1,000 a day, he wasn't even selling half of that. So, I decided to try to incentivize him. I told him that if he sold over $800 on a given day, I'd give him a $50 bonus.

Well, soon enough, he was bringing in over $800 each day. It took me some time to realize what was actually happening. Instead of actually working harder, this employee found ways to fluff up the truckloads with brush and anything else he could find, doubling the price for the customer. In turn, this created a lot of unhappy customers, and my business didn't actually benefit long-term.

When you spot feedback loops like this, you have to change them right away. Otherwise, they will suck your business dry.

Remember: a positive feedback loop will always be a win-win-win. If there's a win-win-lose or win-lose-win, something's off.

CHAPTER 11

MAINTAIN CULTURE

Once you have the right people in place, it's important to set and maintain the culture you desire. In my businesses, everyone is on an equal playing field. I run things very much like a flat organization. In this structure, communication is not based on hierarchy. Respect is given to everyone.

An organization that operates from the top down creates an environment where everyone always looks upward for direction and fears the repercussions of making wrong decisions on their own. In contrast, I look for self-managing individuals. I create boundaries and systems that are clear and easy to follow, but then I encourage employees to take ownership. Yes, I have metrics to ensure that the job is getting done, but for the most part, each staff member manages themselves.

This kind of approach is important to the culture in my businesses. That said, I know plenty of top-down businesses filled with happy staff and a happy CEO. For me, I choose not to hire middle managers and instead return that value to the self managing staff through higher pay. In the end, you have to know what is important to you and then live out that culture. Regardless of where you land with the question of culture, one thing is for sure: you must remove toxicity right away.

REMOVE TOXICITY

Toxic people can be avoided from the very start. Too many business owners hire based on resume, degrees, and experience, even if the person is toxic. Don't do this.

If you don't like someone, don't hire them. That should go without saying, but so many business owners do the opposite. They hire the salesperson who has an amazing track record and sells like crazy but is hated by everyone in the company because they're a jerk. This comes with a cost—a long-term, hidden cost. These people can infect your company and negatively impact the rest of your staff, lessening motivation and overall job satisfaction. When good people are forced to work with idiots, they leave.

Granted, a bad apple slips through here or there, regardless of how much effort you put into your hiring process.

If this happens, you have to be candid with the person. Sit down with them and ask them if you are doing something to elicit their negative feelings about your company. Ask how you can make their job better. Try to find out if they are going through something personally and ask if you can help. Sometimes you'll discover a problem that is solvable.

In one case, I had an employee who had worked with me for

ten years. I could tell something had shifted, so I had a conversation with him. He opened up and shared that he didn't feel appreciated after working so hard for so long. In this case, it was my fault. I had neglected to show my appreciation. So, I bought him a $500 gift card for his family to go out to dinner and made a conscious effort to pop in on jobsites and remind him how thankful I was. Thankfully, this conversation allowed me to keep this employee on board, and both of us were better off for it.

On the flip side, that conversation could end much differently. You might try to get to the bottom of things and realize the person is simply a complainer. That's who they are. Their default is "no." They say no before you even finish the sentence. That's who they are. In other cases, you might discover there is actually something bigger going on with addiction, something you often can't fix for the person. Of course, you always want to approach these situations with compassion and try to offer help. But at some point, you may realize there is no more you are able to do and that the person will need to choose to change themselves.

In these kinds of cases, you have to let the person go. A toxic employee will infect your company like a virus, and it's very difficult to undo the damage.

PASSING DOWN CULTURE

While I use the flat organizational structure in my businesses, I do take a "top-down" approach in one area: leading by example.

This is one of the best ways to maintain the culture you want in your company. And it starts with the small things.

A few weeks ago, one of my employees called and said he had an emergency and would have to take the weekend off to help his family move. This put me in a difficult position, as I now had to find someone to cover for him. But rather than responding with my frustration, I tried to empathize with his situation.

"I'm sorry you're going through that," I said. "That must be terrible for your family. Don't worry about it. I've got this." The truth was I didn't "have this." In fact, I was now in a difficult situation, but nowhere near as difficult as his. "No" wasn't an option, so why bother him with my issues?

When that employee came back to work, I noticed his attitude was back to 100 percent. He was ready to get to work, and his positive energy was infectious.

This is the power of creating a culture from the top down and being the example first. When you follow the simple golden rule, most people will respond. They, too, will then treat other employees and customers with the same respect.

Many companies have long lists of values and a lot of words to explain their culture. While this can be helpful, you can also keep things simple. Work with principles of care and respect. If you start there and others follow your example, there is little else you'll have to do to maintain the positive culture you want in the company.

Take some time to determine what values matter most to you. Then be the example. Live out those values, and see how others take your lead.

CHAPTER 12

EMPOWER YOUR PEOPLE WITH SYSTEMS

As your business gets early traction, you will start to add all of the obvious systems, such as payroll, bookkeeping, HR, inter-staff communication, and more. As your business grows and you create jobs, you begin to realize all the not-so-obvious systems you need to truly empower your people.

For example, how does your company deal with logins to your online tools? What happens to those logins when a person leaves the company? How do you ensure that the passwords don't get exploited by outsiders?

Maybe you run a coffee shop where the restroom is being used by non-customers. You'll need a lock with a key or keypad. Who controls these? How often will you change the code? Do you have a backup key?

Do you have a trucking company with 20 trucks and keys? Who

controls them? How many copies should you have? Where should they be stored? Should your employees take them home? How about your truck's cleanliness? Should you wash them daily as they come in? Who manages the pressure washers, fuel, hoses, and maintenance? Do you have a person who comes in at the end of the day to spray them all down?

Maybe you use uniforms in your business. How often should these be replaced? What's to be done in the case of damage? How many shirts does each employee need? Who's responsible for buying them?

These examples might sound trivial, but without systems in place, they will turn into big problems down the road for those who run things on a day-to-day basis. If you tell yourself these things will just get done when needed, your employees will be stuck with the problem. Don't let this happen. Remember, the responsibility must start with you.

Set up your systems now and empower your people for the long term.

MAKE YOURSELF USELESS

Whether it was in the Army or working at one of the many jobs I've had in my life, the purpose was always to be as useful as possible. Naturally, once I was a business owner, this idea carried over, and the idea of being useless didn't sit right with me.

But what about when your "usefulness" starts to get in the way? If you're not present, can the business run? The answer should be a big YES.

When you started your business, you wore all of the hats, but now you have to take those hats off and hand them to others.

This process reminds me of the first time I dropped my son off at preschool. My wife and I work from home and spend all of our time with him. The thought went through my mind: *Surely, I can't just drop him off to complete strangers! He'll perish!*

But we, of course, did drop him off, albeit nervously. And to our surprise, he was smiling when we came to pick him up at the end of the day. My visions of the puffy eyes and tears and hunger were all in my head; they weren't real.

Sure, we could have simply chosen not to take this step. We could have kept him home, away from the other kids. We could have stunted his personal growth to remain comfortable. But we chose to move past the discomfort and let go.

And this is exactly what you have to do with your company.

Your job is ultimately to make yourself useless to your company. If you feel like you have a job, then it's time to either create better systems or hire someone new to take tasks away from you. In the 1 to 2 phase, your only job is to make your company run seamlessly, so you can sit in the background and envision the direction, the growth, the next company acquisition, or simply take more time with your family.

If you don't learn to make yourself useless, you'll just keep running payroll, keep answering calls, and keep using all your time to land the next big account. And in turn, your company will stall out.

It's time to let go. It's time to empower your people.

START HERE

If you aren't sure where to start with systems, here are a few categories to focus on first.

- Software solutions
- Hiring and personnel
- Customer Service and feedback loops
- Metrics tracking and triggers (see Chapter 16)
- Marketing automation
- Standard Operating Procedures (SOPs)

Now that we've talked about amplifying yourself by leveraging people, it's time to take things to the next level. Let's look at next-level tactics and systems you can start using today.

NEXT-LEVEL TACTICS

Once you've built a solid foundation beneath your business, it's time to focus on the form and function—creating a business that works for you, even if you're spending time with family, working on another business, or sleeping. It should always be serving you.

Abraham Lincoln famously said, "If you give me six hours to cut down a tree, I'll spend the first four hours sharpening the axe." Too many entrepreneurs are chopping feverishly at their tree because they haven't taken the time to sharpen their axe. This is the guy who went from zero to one but can't shift up. Stopping to sharpen the axe at this point is critical.

In this part of the book, we look at strategic moves that can take you to the next level in your thinking and doing. This is where you truly sharpen your axe and set your business (and yourself) apart.

CHAPTER 13

ELIMINATE FIRST

Years ago, I did dispatch for my hauling company and came up with a simple tracking system. At the time, I had ten trucks going out on a consistent basis. So, I'd number them one to ten in a paper scheduler and list the jobs and times below each. When a truck was en route, I'd circle the address they were headed to. When the job was in progress, I'd put one line through it, and when it was complete, I'd add a line to create an X. I'd then mark how much of their truck was filled up so I would know what the remaining capacity was for more jobs before having to head to the dumps.

The entire process was extremely simple, but it worked.

Eventually, a software company hounded me enough that they sold me on a fancy dispatch system. It ended up being a total disaster.

The level of complexity that was required to train staff, customers, and vendors far exceeded the value of the software. I learned an important lesson through this experience: *know your business and make choices according to what your business actually is and where you actually are.*

If you are running a million-dollar business, you don't need billion-dollar solutions. Scaling is important, but a system that can handle a thousand customers per minute is unnecessary if you currently handle a thousand customers per year. Don't be sold on the Silicon Valley blitz scaling mentality. Keep it simple and find scaling solutions that simplify your workload and have the capacity to scale 5-10X.

The simpler your systems are, the easier it will be to pivot and grow your business. When you do get to the point where you need the more complex system, it will still be there. And you can certainly rest assured that someone will still be ready to sell it to you. By that time, your needs may have changed anyway.

Often when I'm talking to business owners, their default thinking is: *What can I add to my business to make it run smoother? Who can I hire? What business should I acquire? Where should I open my next location?*

There is always time for these questions, but the first step is to focus on creating a lean, mean version of your existing business. Once you can't take away anything else, then you can look to add.

THE BLACK BOX

Ultimately, your business should be a black box where you input staff, advertising, products, and systems, and out the other end comes profit. This box should be extremely elegant. You want to remove all the extra fluff in between or the extra pipes sticking out.

In many ways, this is like getting your business into flow state. And you simply can't do that when you over-complicate everything in the business. One of the main ways I see business owners overcomplicate things is by focusing on the extra things instead of the core things. They simply can't see what matters most.

Recently, I started helping someone in the crypto space. He has already spent thousands on traffic to his website, but there's just one problem: the website doesn't convert.

Finally, I got him to see the problem. It's as if he's hiring drivers to bring people to his restaurant, while the restaurant has graffitied windows and a homeless guy is set up right outside the front door. He's spending so much effort on what doesn't matter that he's missing the point. He has no chance of building an elegant black box because his priorities are all off.

Sometimes, entrepreneurs keep themselves busy with all the things that don't really matter because they don't want to face the main issues in their business. But this avoidance doesn't help anyone, and it certainly doesn't lead to a flow state. It simply keeps you running around in circles with zero results. If you find yourself in this state, start by simplifying. Focus on the main problem, then go from there.

LEGACY SYSTEMS, LEGACY MINDSET

In some cases, business owners are actually held back because they aren't willing to innovate and move forward. They're stuck in the past. Of course, this happens all the time in all kinds of contexts.

I was recently talking to my friend who is a firefighter, and he was explaining how it's so frustrating when they send out Zoom call invites because, inevitably, someone will lose the email and be reaching out to him last minute. When I asked him why they haven't found a better way to share the Zoom link, such as setting up a messaging system, he said, "It's just the way it's always been done."

Whenever I hear that phrase, I know it's time for some reassessment. It brings me right back to the way the military operated. This kind of thinking doesn't actually streamline anything. What needs to be eliminated in this case is the legacy mindset and the legacy system so that something new can replace both.

As a scrappy, bootstrapped business owner, you know what it's like to find solutions that work and get the job done. But the truth is that many of the systems you set up when you were getting your business off the ground may now be a hindrance to your business as it grows. Just because it worked then doesn't mean it's working now.

When I opened my first electronics recycling center, we would have customers fill out a piece of paper to prove that the CRT or TV came from California to avoid fraud. These forms allowed us to be reimbursed by the State. At the end of the day, I would have a member of my staff enter these into a spreadsheet that we would submit to the State. This was a great system when we had ten to twenty drop-offs per day, but when we started having hundreds of drop-offs per day at multiple locations, the paperwork became overwhelming.

I could have thrown up my hands and said, "Well, that's the way we've always done it." But I didn't. I examined our systems and devised a new one where the client would fill out a Google form on a tablet. When they hit submit, the form would feed into a spreadsheet. This saved hours of labor and lots of transcription errors.

If it makes sense to use new technologies as your company grows, do it. But remember, this shift should ultimately help you eliminate and simplify. Notice I didn't have to hire a software development company to create an expensive scaling solution. Had I continued to grow, I could have hired a developer to create a more robust system based on my Google doc, but even then, the goal would be to streamline the business, not to make it more complicated.

THE NEW AND FANCY

Too many business owners are sold on what's new but isn't useful. Just because something looks fancy doesn't mean it's the best.

Over time, I've learned there are a lot of snake oil salesmen out there trying to huck the latest and greatest solution. Whether it be blockchain, social media, CRM software, Artificial Intelligence, Internet of things, or all of the other buzzwords.

But can these things actually help your business where it is right now? Is it necessary to tokenize your business because a crypto bro says so? Do you need a full-time Social Media manager if you sell a highly specialized product with a very narrow demographic of buyers? How complicated does your CRM software have to be if you only have a handful of clients paying you 6 figures each? Can you get something more from complicated artificial intelligence that you can't get from polling your customers?

Sure, all of these solutions have a place in the market, but only you (not the salesperson) can evaluate if they have a place in your business. There's a reason SaaS salespeople go after funded startups. They know they have no financial discipline. This isn't you. You have to be financially disciplined to escape The Hustle Trap.

START SHEDDING

Take time to evaluate legacy systems or where you're considering what's new and shiny. Can you simplify your life by shedding instead?

You want to always be on the lookout for ways to simplify your business. This is part of your role now that you are done with hustling. It's up to you to make your business run like it's in flow state all of the time.

Of course, simplifying can take on many forms. With technology advances, new solutions arrive that may not have been affordable before but can now help you manage your business in a new way.

Many solutions can also integrate several of your systems into one. You might have a time tracking system for employees, a GPS system to track vehicles, and a billing system to bill your customers hourly. If you find new software that bills your customers automatically based on real-time GPS that will only allow your employees to log in within a geofenced area to prevent padding the clock, it's worth at least taking a look. These kinds of all-in-one solutions aren't simply shiny objects. If they can increase productivity and decrease cost substantially, they're actual solutions.

To know if something is worth adding to your business, consider how it helps you eliminate. Ask: *Will it save time? Will it help us avoid mistakes? Will it save labor? Will it save money? Or is it just pretty and new?*

CHAPTER 14

KNOW HOW TO "NO"

In my drafting company, we keep everything in Google. That makes our lives easier and keeps things streamlined. Recently, a customer wanted to bring my architect into Asana because that was how they communicated. When I said no, they pushed back, threatening to take their business elsewhere.

I responded by saying I was sorry we couldn't do business with them, and finally, they changed their minds. They would make it work for us.

This was one of the many times I had to say no to a customer trying to pull me into their world. In each case, I've learned to draw them into mine.

Don't get me wrong. I love making my customers happy, but there's a line that needs to be drawn. Sometimes customers have their own way of doing things that, if accommodated, will throw off your well-oiled machine.

Throughout the years, I've had customers try to pull me into their billing systems, their communication tools, their software systems, and a swath of other systems that are incompatible with mine. Every time I've made exceptions for these customers, it has added unnecessary complications and negatively affected my productivity.

Sure, there are always exceptions to the rule, and you should create systems around those. For example, large corporations often have their own payment systems that they must use. Government contracts have to be structured very specifically. High-security projects require special protocols and clearances.

But for the most part, you can establish your non-negotiables and stick to them. I own a digital service business that does not do any billing. We only accept payment upfront for services provided. I've had several companies over the years ask to set up an account and pay on Net 30 terms. If a customer ever starts with, "We need to set up an account and get you set up in our system to get you paid," I keep my response simple: "All payments are made upfront through our website." If they say, "We only make payments on Net 30," I respond, "Oh, I'm sorry to hear that. We were really looking forward to working with you." Oftentimes, we'll get an order from that customer the following day, done through our website on our terms.

Had I accepted the Net 30 terms, I would have had to set up accounts receivable, collections, and job tracking systems—just for that one customer. This would take manpower, and people aren't cheap. By not allowing customers to work on their terms, I've saved a lot of money and kept my business simple.

A TIME SUCK

There was a point in 2008 when the housing market crashed, and foreclosures were on the rise. Banks were in need of people to preserve their foreclosed properties. Since I had recently had my accident and wanted to keep my guys working, I thought this was a perfect opportunity.

The only problem was that some of the banks wanted to pay 90-180 days after the work was done. This put me into a serious cash crunch, and when the 90 days came, I'd still have to spend my days working through the banking channels trying to get payment.

Their response was even worse. They explained that because they were such a big company and continually feeding us with work, we would have to be patient with payment. After months of fighting, I finally got paid. After that, I was done, so I told them they would have to pay all jobs with a credit card on the day of the jobs. I knew they wouldn't be willing to do this, but I gave them a chance. Sure enough, they refused, and we parted ways. I was happy for my competitors to deal with them while I spent more time servicing our good customers.

This experience taught me a lot. In particular, it taught me how important it is to have clearly defined processes and nonnegotiables. These end up saving you a lot of time in the long run.

HURTING OTHER CUSTOMERS

The other unintended consequence of allowing customers to interrupt your systems is that it takes time away from other customers. If your employees are having to log into a separate system to communicate with the client, then they are not on their normal channels to service others.

There's a switching cost that goes into moving between different systems. If you have all of your customers communicating through Slack and then one customer wants to use Asana, you will now have to go back and forth, causing downtime in Slack. Don't fall for this trap. As soon as you allow this, everyone will start to pull you into their systems, and you will not be able to grow your business.

CLARIFY YOUR BOUNDARIES

Setting boundaries around your systems will protect your company and your time. So what are your boundaries, and how do you establish them? It really depends on your industry and company size.

If I don't get my order on time from Amazon, can I call Jeff Bezos and ask why? No. I can't even call Amazon. I have to go through their specified channels to get a resolution. If you're a pool maintenance company, on the other hand, you want simpler channels to reach you in the event of an issue. If you're a one-man operator, it might be your cell phone and text. If you have an office receptionist, then they would be the point of contact so your field people can focus on getting work done without having to stop to take calls. In this case, you might have a company policy that employees cannot give their phone number to customers. All calls, chats, and emails must go through a single point of contact in your office. The office person can then connect them to the correct person in the company.

This is a simple concept, but I constantly see small companies that let customers call the service people directly. As a result, the service person either pulls over on the side of the road or stops sweeping a pool to take a call, leading to decreased productivity. "Sorry, company policy doesn't allow me to give out my cell phone number, but if you call the office, they can always get ahold of me. Here's that number." It's that simple.

If you don't know what your boundaries are, you can't be firm on your "no." So, start there.

CHAPTER 15

FROM PROBLEM TO SYSTEM

As my demolition company grew, I noticed that drivers started calling more and more to talk through every little issue. Oftentimes, it was something as simple as not being able to move a piece of concrete because it was too big.

Whenever they'd call with this kind of issue, I'd always ask a number of questions. *Did you try a sledgehammer?* No. *Did you try lifting it up and then using a sledgehammer?* No. *Did you try backing the truck up next to it to use that as leverage?* No.

Why were the answers no? Because they were simply waiting for someone to come help them.

Eventually, the calls were taking too much of my time, and I knew I had to come up with a simple system to put ownership back onto my people. So, I came up with The Rule of Three: *you can call me, but you have to tell me three things you've already tried.*

After implementing this protocol, calls dropped by 90 percent.

I still told everyone they were free to call me, but they knew the first thing I would ask for were the three things they had already tried.

This simple rule shifts an employee's mindset from *How can you help me?* to *How can I help myself?*

I've found that once employees take it upon themselves to look for solutions, they'll try more than three things. Once the ego is involved, they want to come up with the solution so they can feel a sense of pride about their accomplishment. At the end of the day, many of my employees started coming to the office and telling me about the difficult situations they had and the creative solution they came up with. I would hear about the way somebody had used a chain around a tree to pull a Bobcat out and then have an opportunity to show appreciation for handling the problem. This new way of handling things turned into an ethos in the company. We are a "Get shit done" company filled with *doers*.

These simple conversations at the end of the day also help in another way. They help you realize more of the problems that can be fixed by creating systems. Over time, for example, enough guys told me about ways they had to fix issues with hydraulic hoses that would blow that I realized each truck should have an extra long hose in it to temporarily fix the problem. Simple as that. The open conversations allowed us to be clear about the problems in the business.

THE SWITCHING COST

Going from being in the middle of doing something to having

to switch to a problem completely alters your focus. So, while a call might only take five minutes, it could take another thirty minutes to refocus on what you were doing before the call.

Clearly, without the constant interruptions, you can save a lot of time each week.

So many business owners will languish in inefficiencies, all the while being frustrated with their people. They might say, "Why don't you try something different?" but they never formalize a rule or system.

Remember, your frustrations should be a sign for what is missing. It should be your prompt.

If you're dealing with constantly switching between tasks every day, be aware of the real cost. It makes sense that you're frustrated. Now it's time to figure out a solution and formalize it. You can start with The Rule of Three, but don't stop there.

What are your other frustrations? Now, what are the creative solutions?

WHEN PROBLEMS AREN'T IMMEDIATELY APPARENT

One year, I discovered a huge blunder we had made when one of our customers told me they had called and left a voicemail, and we never responded. I thought, *Really, wouldn't we have known about that?*

Well, as it turned out, we didn't know about that call and another 400 or so calls, which had all been forwarded to a cloud-based system. Later, we realized what had happened. If someone was on the phone, and a second call came in, it would go to voicemail. However, if a third call came in, it would go to this cloud-based system.

Unfortunately, the problem hadn't gotten big enough to notice until I started answering the phone. My office manager said they had heard a couple of complaints, but they assumed someone else had listened to the voicemail or it got deleted accidentally.

Once we finally discovered the problem, we fixed it immediately by creating a system that actually worked. In this case, we put all voicemails straight to the cloud-based system and then checked that platform frequently.

It was a stupid mistake but easily overlooked in the day-to-day chaos of running a small business. Unfortunately, this little mistake likely cost tens of thousands of dollars in lost sales.

When you reframe mistakes, problems, inefficiencies, and frustrations into a lack of systems, you start to look at your business in a new way. For the voicemail problem, there were plenty of opportunities to uncover this early on, but there were no systems to catch it. Had I created a log of customer issues that was kept by my customer service staff, it would have been noted that customers were complaining about not getting calls back when they left a voicemail. This would have been worth investigating and could have easily been fixed. Instead, my customer service staff would just say something like, "I apologize for someone not getting back to you. That's not usual." They then would carry on with the conversation.

Today, I have someone on my staff do chat and phone audits weekly. Their job is to listen to every recorded call and read every chat. They take notes on areas of improvement, recurring customer concerns, and whether the customer got the answers they were looking for in an efficient and fast way. By having this system in place, I proactively avoid a lot of issues that might occur in the future and provide a better customer experience.

KEEP AN OPEN CONVERSATION

Problems happen. Mistakes also happen. These should be expected parts of any business.

I recently had an employee confess that she made a big mistake that was totally avoidable. This is a staff member who I know truly cares about my company and our customers.

After she shared, I said, "Look, if you aren't making mistakes, you aren't working fast enough. Carry on." And she did.

Responses like this set the culture in your company. Micromanaged employees are incredibly inefficient. If your employees are consumed with achieving perfection, their work will actually suffer. If they know they can be candid about mistakes, they'll be much more likely to keep hustling and figure out what needs to be fixed as they go.

You can't fix issues you don't know about. You want to create an environment that allows the issues to surface. Whenever an employee tells me about a mistake they've made, I thank them for telling me and then try to make light of it. At the same time,

I look to see if the reason it happened was due to a lack of a system. After all, everything is my fault!

If I can create another system so that other employees don't make the same mistake, I will. That's on me.

CHAPTER 16

TRACK METRICS

Numbers matter. And you must get to know the numbers that matter for your business. Be careful, though, about singling out any specific metric. As an aggregate, they are important, but if you focus solely on profitability, user growth, or gross revenue, it will almost always backfire.

Many startups are only concerned with the KPI (key performance indicator) of user growth or gross revenue. A couple of years ago, a startup made big waves with a service that brought refueling to your house for a minimal fee. When I looked at the numbers, however, they didn't add up. When I ran a trucking company that used over 500 gallons a day of diesel, I couldn't find a delivery service for the "low volume" request we had.

This company did gain users, but I knew there was no way they could be profitable. Sure enough, their prices skyrocketed once they repriced the service for profitability, and they went under. Their focus was solely on user growth.

Uber has faced similar issues of trying to balance user growth with profitability.

Some companies that only focus on short-term profitability, on the other hand, forget to think about the customer and building a long-term relationship with them. Soon enough, their reputation is shot, and it's extremely difficult to recover from a bad reputation.

I have tended to focus on customer lifetime value in my businesses. All of my businesses have succeeded solely on the satisfaction of my customers. The longer they remain a customer, the more they spend and the less I have to spend on marketing. Long-term customers are also more likely to refer my business to friends and colleagues.

TRIGGERS

Instead of KPIs, I use triggers to track important metrics.

Every company is different, and your mix of triggers needs to be relevant for you. For my online digital service business, I look at a list of daily metrics. If something is off, it's a simple trigger for me. I focus on conversion rate, revenue, ad spend, traffic, site visits, new versus repeating customers, order count, and average customer star rating. I know these numbers inside and out because I review them every morning.

I know, for example, that a healthy conversion rate for the business is 4 percent. If one day I see that the conversion rate is at 2 percent, I can immediately look into the issue. On one hand, I might find that we had a recent spike in non-targeted traffic to the site. When I look at Google, I find that an article linked to us, and because of the way it was phrased, our services seemed relevant to the reader, even though they weren't. Naturally, this would cause a decrease in the conversion rate. Nonetheless, I appreciate the traffic, but it's a nonissue.

On the other hand, I might find that there is actually a bug in the checkout process for certain browsers. Or there might be an issue on the site where people can't include their address, so they give up and leave. In these cases, I have to be on the issue right away. There's absolutely no reason not to catch that issue or let it linger.

A star rating drop might not sound as important as conversion rate, but in many businesses, it is. Reputation can make or break you. If our average rating is 4.8, and I see that our weekly average drops to 4.2, I know there's a problem and want to figure out the issue fast. This is such an important part of our business that it is bound to affect sales, profitability, and long-term growth.

I might find that one of the chat representatives has had a bad week. I can back this up with data from the numbers, and it's an easy conversation. "Hey, it looks like your star rating went down from 4.8 to 3.5 last week. In reviewing the chats, it seems like some of your answers weren't quite on point. So, let's go through some retraining to get the rating back where it should be." It's an easy conversation to have, but it wouldn't be effective without a trigger or without the numbers to back up what's happening right now.

On a monthly basis, I'll look at metrics such as customer

lifetime value, return on ad spend, discount code usage, and customer churn. What you want to know is whether the mean is staying steady or improving. If it's not, that's when you dive in deeper and see what's going on.

START HERE

Your triggers and the metrics you look at are going to be determined by the business you run. If you run a hauling business, for example, you might be less concerned with chat ratings. You may not even have a chat function available. What you would be concerned about is your labor cost or your fuel cost per day. What's amazing about the time we live in is that all of this can be automated. This is where you want to use technology to your advantage to simplify your life.

One way to start building out the right triggers for your business is by listing out the top ten metrics you need to track in your business. Categorize these into daily and monthly metrics. Then, once you have these in place, you will know what triggers you need to set up for yourself. You'll need to put in some upfront work here. This might feel like you're going backwards to hustling, but you're not.

I use a software called Glew that takes data from dozens of sources such as Google Analytics, Google Ads, email, and Quickbooks. From there, I select the most relevant triggers and put them into a daily email digest that I review every morning. Each number is a trigger for my business and gives me the overall health of the company.

A trigger lets you know something is off. It's like taking your temperature and realizing you have a fever. You know something is off and need to investigate further. My triggers help me do the same with my business.

This is a high-level task to refine your processes and move your business to the next level. Yes, it will take a bit of work to set up Google Analytics, Google Alerts, or an app that tracks daily fuel usage, but the effort is minimal compared to the payoff. You will thank yourself for taking this step, and your business will thank you too.

CHAPTER 17

FIND YOUR EDGE

I once had a conversation with the CEO of a large grocery chain. He told me it was much more difficult to run a large publicly traded company because all eyes were always on him, whereas the smaller grocery chains could get away with so much more. Some of them would spray their fruits and vegetables to add more weight and, as a result, charge more money. As the leader in the space, he simply couldn't get away with the same thing.

Our conversation made me think of all of the ways I can use the smaller size of my company to my advantage.

When I began to focus almost exclusively on swimming pool removal, I had to think fast because a lot of my competitors were looking at me and right on my tail. Soon enough, they'd be taking away my business unless I could find a choke point that I could control to lock the rest out.

What I found was that dirt was the choke point. If you don't have dirt, you can't fill a swimming pool. But if you control the dirt, no one can catch you. If you couldn't get dirt in a timely manner, the only option was to buy the dirt from a fill provider, and this could be very costly. If you could only bring in a load or two a day, the job would take forever, and the neighbors would start to complain about the noise and dirt tracking down the street. I wasn't willing to add this cost or wait weeks to have a pool filled.

So, I went a different route. I began to network with all of the truckers and excavators who worked on jobsites in the Bay area. I told them that if they had dirt, we had a place for it. If I didn't have a pool close to their jobsite, I would find them a dumpsite somewhere else as long as it wasn't for a competitor. Within a short amount of time, I was filling swimming pools in a single day, while my competitors would take several days or even weeks.

Not only did I have happier customers, but I was making more than anyone else. And ultimately, my new network actually led to a whole new business, an online dirt exchange I called Dirt Match.

Every business I've ever owned has had an edge that kept me above the competition. What's your edge?

BE STRATEGIC

To find your edge, you have to find creative ways to give your business the advantage. You have to find a way to take up space.

I did this quite literally with my hauling business when I realized a way to get a full-page ad in the Yellow Pages where none of my competitors could.

In the Yellow Pages, they put hauling in the "Rubbish Removal" section. If someone went to "H," they would see a note that said, "Hauling, refer to Rubbish Removal." They'd have to flip all the way to "R" before they'd see the ad. So, I decided to make my business a "Hauling and Hat company." Soon enough, I had my business listed right there in "H," set apart from everyone.

The following year, PacBell Yellow Pages told me I couldn't do this again, so I simply went to their competitor—Valley Yellow Pages. They were a smaller company with less bureaucracy, so I told them I'd pay $10,000 per month to have a full-page ad in "Hauling" if they agreed to open that section up for my category. They agreed, so I went back to the PacBell Yellow Pages to use this as leverage. "Valley Yellow Pages agreed," I said. "What do you think?"

Soon enough, I had my full-page ad right there in "Hauling" in both of the big books. This decision was made after the submission deadline, so my competitors were still buried under the Rubbish section while I took 100 percent of the business.

Within the next couple of years, everything was transitioning online, so I had to adapt again. I told the Yellow Pages that I was only willing to pay per call. They agreed to give me a unique phone number and charge me $3 per call. The call volume was so low that I ended up getting the $10,000 per month ad for around $60 per month. That was my last year in the Yellow Pages. In the meantime, I was the only "Hauling" advertiser on Google Adwords, paying pennies per click.

This is all part of the game. No matter what kind of business you have, you have to be willing and able to adapt consistently to stay ahead of your competition.

Today, I'm willing to spend up to the full cost of the sale to acquire new customers and then provide amazing customer service to keep them coming back. I only make money on the second sale and beyond, and I'm completely okay with this. I know that 30 percent of my customers will turn into repeats, so it's a long-term success plan. The level of customer service I provide is unparalleled in the industry, so my competitors, who are forced to pay more to acquire a customer and convert far less into repeats, struggle to make a profit. The upfront cost is worth it to essentially own the space I want to own.

Take some time to consider how you can be strategic in your own business. Where is your edge, doing what no one else has thought to do? What will be your advantage? How can you make your competition compete on your terms? And how do you keep that edge?

CHAPTER 18

GAMIFY YOUR TIME

After a couple of years of being in business, another business owner encouraged me to set my time's worth. So, I gave it a try.

At the time, I decided that my time was worth $50 an hour. This changed a lot of how I approached what I did and what I outsourced to others. If someone was willing to mow my lawn for $15, I couldn't do that task any longer. If I was spending two hours writing a blog post, whereas someone else can write it in an hour for $50 total, I had to stop writing my posts.

Over time, I began to shed more and more, and I also began to gamify my time.

What if I valued my time at $100 an hour, then $500 an hour? Today, I won't do anything for less than $1,000 an hour.

What is even more interesting is to look at how much you can make while doing even less work. This is the goal, remember?

In one of my online businesses, for example, I often spend a total of thirty minutes a week on it. I'll check my metrics, and I might have a short conversation with my customer service manager. Some weeks, the business brings in $25,000 in profit. So, in essence, I'm making $50,000 per hour.

This is a fun game to play, but more importantly, it allows you to truthfully examine how much you're progressing in escaping The Hustle Trap and building out a true cash machine—that Black Box that spits out your welfare check each week.

THE FLIPSIDE

Many entrepreneurs—rather than gamifying their time and becoming more efficient—actually become busier because they let people take advantage of their time.

It's critical to understand that *people won't respect your time; you have to make them respect it.*

Having digital boundaries is especially important today. I typically won't check or respond to emails after noon each day, and prior to noon, I only check my email every two hours. This goes back to the switching cost problem. If you're switching your focus to random emails every thirty minutes, you are essentially allowing others to monopolize your time.

I'm regularly pulled into meetings on Zoom for a variety of projects. Most of these meetings start off with small talk, and then everyone throws ideas around for an hour before coming to a conclusion that no one will act on. When I started looking at the outcomes of the meetings, I found that about 5 percent of the meeting had the information, and 95 percent was swirling around irrelevant topics.

Now when I get invited to a Zoom meeting, I send my assistant to take notes. I ask that a recording be sent to me, and I have my assistant mark any time stamps where she thinks I should listen. Once the meeting is sent to me, I review the notes and any time-stamped sections and then reply to the group with any of my input. This whole process usually takes me five minutes or less. If my attendance is required, I still bring my VA to take notes so I can multitask during the meeting.

Zoom meetings aren't the worst of it, either. Some people want to meet in person for discussion. Unless it's a good friend, I will always respond with a big NO. Recently, I had someone in my CEO group ask if I could meet with him and his Operations Officer to "pick my brain." Not a very nice saying, but okay. If you want to pick my brain, you have to at least be willing to put in the effort on your end.

I told him that I go on afternoon hikes in Griffith Park regularly, and he could join me for one. He didn't respond.

He wanted me to drive an hour out to Venice (from Hollywood) to pick my brain. No thanks.

Obviously, each response will depend on the person and your level of connection to them. But even for close connections, you can find a different way. You could say, "I'll call you on my way home from work for a quick discussion." Or "I'm not free, but let's get you on a Zoom call with my assistant so I can get a better feel for your proposal." Or "I have to pick up my dry cleaning at 11 a.m. There's a coffee shop next door, and I could chat there until 11:15."

The point is to put their request back on them. They need to be the one putting in the effort. They need to be prepared to be efficient in the discussion. If they aren't willing to do this, they aren't actually willing to invest in themselves.

Remember: an open-ended meeting is the death of your time. Don't do it!

KNOW YOUR WORTH

The deeper principle here is to value your time. Know your worth and evaluate all of your decisions through this.

I find that so many entrepreneurs, even the smartest ones, don't do this.

Recently, my friend offered a perfect example on this front. He told me he was considering buying a business for $10,000. He explained that it brought in $1,000 a month. From that viewpoint, it seemed like it might be a smart investment, but then I dug deeper.

I came to find out that he would have to put in at least two hours a day to make the thing work. I did a little math with him and said, "Do you really want to buy this business just to make $16 an hour? You can make more than that at Starbucks, and you don't even have to pay them to get started."

We laughed together, but the conversation was revealing. This particular friend is brilliant and has had a wildly successful corporate career. And yet he was ready to value his time at $16 an hour.

Don't do this.

Your time needs to go to what is most valuable only—to those things that lead to the greatest results. When you start practicing a new way to work with your time, that's when you will truly start to live life "on the other side," as we'll see in Part 4.

LIFE ON THIS SIDE

Now that the roadblocks are removed, it's time to clear the path for your business to work for you.

If you can master the skills outlined in the first three parts of the book, you will emerge as a different kind of entrepreneur—one who peers into his business from the outside without the clouded judgment of a business owner buried in the day-to-day. You will know how to make money with your mind, not your time. Let's explore this life on the other side and what it looks like.

CHAPTER 19

OPTIMIZE FOR INDEPENDENCE AND AUTONOMY

As entrepreneurs, we break out on our own and leave the security of an employer in hopes of creating something better for ourselves. Sadly, too many entrepreneurs end up slaves to their own businesses, working more hours, taking on more responsibilities over time, and often end up making less money.

It's an easy trap to fall into if you aren't intentional about creating an environment of freedom and autonomy for yourself. Every aspect of your business needs to be modeled for this purpose. Every new hire, new service area, new equipment, or new system should be examined to make sure it accomplishes this. *How will X buy me more freedom while helping to grow my business?*

This also applies to all current systems and people in your business. *How is this person helping to give me freedom so that I can focus on what's important? How is this system freeing me from the day-to-day operations of my business?*

Only when you examine every aspect of your business to ensure it aligns with your goal of freedom will you be able to focus on growth.

Too many entrepreneurs think they have to make sweeping changes with every decision. In many cases, investing in the small things is what goes the furthest. If you're not willing to invest two hours of time to save ten minutes a day, you won't reach the level of autonomy you want. It's all the details, after all, that suck away your time and energy.

START SMALL

There was a time when all of my employees would come back to the office at the end of the day and drop off a handful of papers for myself or my office manager to enter into a computer system. This was an arduous task and before many of the new digital solutions were available. We would spend an hour or two entering this data manually.

Since we had paperwork from 10-12 individuals, it finally occurred to me that if they all entered their own information, it would only take them 10 minutes each rather than the hour or two it would take me. I created a simple form in Google docs that fed into a shared database. Each employee would enter their own information, and suddenly my office manager and I were free from this task.

These types of efficiencies can hide in plain sight if you don't pay attention, and often they are present because you are not empowering your people to complete tasks on their own. The more you can rely on your people, the more freedom you will have to work on more important parts of your business or life.

Remember: *your job is to not have a job.*

You should have ZERO daily tasks after you review your critical metrics. Everything should be on your time. You might love to make sales, manage your people, or spend time at your office. That's all fine and good, but you shouldn't *have* to do any of it.

ALARM CLOCKS SUCK

Using an alarm clock is an admission that you are not in control. An alarm clock starts your day in a reactionary state. To wake up whenever is best for you, you have to have true independence from your business tasks.

Create a life where you can always follow your inspiration. If you find yourself inspired at 11:00 p.m. and get into your zone of genius, the last thing you want to do is shut it down because you have to wake up for work at 6:00 a.m. If you wake up naturally when you're rested, you will be more productive in your day and get more done. Your mind will be more clear, and you'll be a better leader in your company and in your life.

I'm not saying you have to give up your morning routines. Morning routines are great if they don't get in the way of your rest. I have friends who have very strict morning routines: wake up at 5:00 a.m., make the bed, run 4 miles, meditate for 20 minutes, shower, eat breakfast, read the news, and then head to work at 7:00 a.m.

This routine works great for them because they naturally wake up at 5:00 a.m. But if you're dragging yourself out of bed, you need to stop. The rest is far more important.

I usually wake up between 4:00 and 5:30 a.m., naturally. When I wake up, I typically just relax and think about the day ahead while I enjoy a cup of coffee. I try to wake up my body by doing some pull-ups or push-ups. I leave the house around 6:30 a.m. and head to the beach to walk for an hour. I'll either walk with my thoughts or a podcast that interests me. This is when my mind prepares itself for the day.

Often a theme will emerge during this hour. I'll find myself focusing on efficiencies, customer satisfaction, employee issues, or maybe a needed family vacation. Around 8:00 a.m. I'll get to my office and do some research on the topics that I've been thinking about all morning. If the focus happens to be on customer service, I'll research apps and solutions or solicit feedback from my staff. I create a course of action and deploy it to my people to research solutions. I'll give a deadline to report back with the findings.

When your mind is in the right place by waking up when you want and getting the rest you need, you'll notice how you are actually much more attuned to your business. As an example, I recently noticed a slight dip in my star ratings in one of my companies. I asked one of my employees to create a spreadsheet to track recurring complaints found in reviews and see if we could get to the bottom of the issue.

It turned out that the issue was centered around agents misunderstanding our service. The next step was to have my employee do an audit on the chats to see if they could find specific examples and if there were particular agents that were the root of the problem. It was quickly uncovered that two of my agents were giving conflicting advice to customers. Once we uncovered this issue, we tested all agents and created a retraining program to get them back up to speed. Once the agents were retrained, the star ratings climbed again. Problem solved!

Remember that types of incremental improvements to your business pay massive dividends over time. And believe it or not, getting rid of the alarm can be your first step there.

WORK BACKWARDS

Start by considering how you want to be spending your time. Now, look at how you actually spend your time. How can you optimize? Return to Part 3 to leverage systems. Return to Part 2 to leverage people. And go back all the way to Part 1 if you're still making excuses.

Now ask yourself: *What's my ideal day or week look like?*

Let's pretend there are no constraints put on your day. Your family, business, and finances are in perfect order, and you have no concerns in the world. How would you spend your day?

Write down, in detail, what your day would look like. *What would you do in the morning when you wake up? What would you eat? Would you exercise? Read a novel or business book? Walk alone or with a friend? Socialize? Dinner with friends and family?*

When you write, I want you to imagine that everything that you write down you would be willing to do (almost) every day for the rest of your life. For example, it's unlikely you want to run a marathon for the rest of your life, but you might want to run two miles per day. Likewise, reading for 8 hours a day is unlikely, but reading an hour per day would be a good everyday activity.

Another way to approach this task is to imagine your perfect lifestyle. *What does it include? More time traveling? More time with family?* List out the categories, so you can see more clearly what it is you actually want in your life.

Once you've mapped out your perfect day or perfect lifestyle, imagine what you would need to happen to make these realities. *Would you need more finances? How much? Who would you need to look after your business? Do you have this person yet? Where might you find them?*

Working backward will allow you to create a roadmap to accomplish your perfect day every day.

If you aren't convinced that you can actually have full freedom, I want to challenge you to set a date six months out to completely leave your business and go do something you love. Is it backpacking? Set the date. Is it taking a float plane to a remote lake? Set the date. Is it sailing across the Atlantic? Set the date.

A few years ago, my wife was invited on an all-expenses-paid two-week trip across Alaska—one week over land and one week on a cruise ship. If I went with her, I would have had little or no reception the whole time. This sounded amazing. There was only one problem: I had recently started a new business, and I was in the process of setting up the systems needed to separate myself from it.

But this opportunity was too good to pass up. So, knowing I only had a month to prepare, I got to work. I hired a new office admin and started training them to run the ins and outs of the business. I made it clear that I would be unreachable. I wrote a list of all of the things that could go wrong and created if/then protocols around them. I also made a booklet of standard operating procedures and let everyone know I'd be off the grid for two weeks. Then I left.

When I did check in every few days when we were in bigger cities, I discovered that everything was running seamlessly with only a few hiccups here and there. I realized through this experience just how quickly you can detach from your business if you really want to.

Sometimes, you need to give yourself that deadline. Once you set the date, you figure it out!

Access to the life you want with full independence, autonomy, and freedom is not that far off. Sometimes, you just need a little kick in the ass to make the moves you need to make so you can live from a different place. And sometimes, that kick needs to come from yourself.

CHAPTER 20

SPOT OPPORTUNITY TRAPS

Before you have a successful business, opportunities can be hard to come by, but as you grow and become more successful, opportunities will start to pop up all around you. Many people will want to partner with you or propose new business opportunities to you. New investments will become available to you on a regular basis.

Any of these opportunities might be great, but most will simply consume your time, energy, and money. Over time, you have to be more and more selective.

DO BUSINESS WITH PEOPLE YOU TRUST AND LIKE

One of the most important ways you can be selective is by carefully choosing who you do business with.

This may seem obvious, but an amazing opportunity with a large payout attached can cloud your judgment. You *must* like and trust the people you work with. If someone offers to partner with you on a project that will double the size of your business in the next year, but you're uncomfortable with the person, the situation will only grow worse.

If it's too good to be true, it probably is.

Recently a heavy-hitting internet marketer pitched an investment opportunity to me. *Put in $200K, and make $60K per year cash flow.*

Sounds great, right? Well, when I asked what the risk was, he hesitated. I pried deeper and asked where the payouts were coming from. Again, he hesitated. Ultimately, it came down to the truth. The $60K cash flow was coming from new investors, but he was convinced that the business would take off, which would create substantial equity. This felt like a Ponzi scheme, without the possibility of liquidity of my initial investment since it was an equity investment. It was a hard pass for me.

These situations can seem appealing at face value, and they are—at first—until the scheme crumbles. Once again, this all comes back to who you're doing business with. If you don't trust what they're saying, keep it simple. Stay away. Don't be tempted by shiny new objects and big piles of easy cash. Always dig deeper and ask an uncomfortable amount of questions. If they start to squirm, run.

LOOK OBJECTIVELY

There will come a point in your business when you have to grow past just making your business survive. You'll have to focus on making it thrive. To do this, you have to look objectively at what will actually work for the long run.

Surviving works for a time. Surviving means making every penny you can from anyone who's willing to pay you. I've been there. I spent years doing some of the nastiest, hardest work I can imagine to get my business off the ground. This included burying a dead horse, shoveling human feces from a closet of a lady whose toilet stopped working, and wheelbarrowing 10,000 lbs of dirt uphill into a truck—all by myself.

I was leveraging what I had, and all I had was a strong body and mind. But this state of being and business couldn't last forever. And it simply wasn't repeatable nor highly profitable. On the other hand, loading a truck with household or construction debris and taking it to the dump was much easier work I could train anyone to do. I could make a 70 percent gross margin and expand. Sure enough, my business skyrocketed.

You have to become incredibly objective here. This may seem callous, but it's not. It's simply good business.

Because of the way I look objectively at what is actually in each opportunity for me, I'm able to spend a lot of my time volunteering as a mentor to existing and future entrepreneurs. Most importantly, I'm able to help people leverage what they have into a business that works for them, and this is incredibly rewarding.

In the end, a good entrepreneur knows not to be drawn into an opportunity trap—whether because it's an easy task to do (i.e., weed whacking when you're actually supposed to be running a construction company) or because the opportunity is only beneficial on a financial level (but is connected to something you don't believe in or someone you don't like).

A good entrepreneur will be incredibly selective with their choices each step of the way.

CHAPTER 21

LEVERAGE WHAT'S PROFITABLE AND REPEATABLE

A lot of people say, "Do what you love." I think much differently than this. I have nothing against doing what you love, but whatever you love doing is not necessarily going to turn into a cash flow machine. The idea of building a cash flow business is that it frees you from having to work, and then you can go do what you love on your own terms. It makes no sense to spoil your passions by burdening them with the demands of a business.

Instead, I do the things I can do, and even sometimes things I hate doing, so that I can build something profitable and repeatable. And once I do, I love it. Not only does the business provide me with freedom, but it also provides a lot of other people with jobs, as I mentioned in the last chapter.

Oftentimes, there is a period of experimentation necessary to find exactly what is most profitable and repeatable, but once you do, you have to stick to it. What all of my businesses have in common is that they are a niche. After a period of trying out a bunch of different things, we honed in on one specific task, which made us all the money and could be easily duplicated over and over again.

For the hauling company, the focus became hauling debris. Period. Not moving, not weed whacking, not delivery. Hauling debris. It was through that business I learned just how important it is to stay focused on the money-making task.

With the demolition company, I didn't truly arrive at a focus until we started the pool removals. With regular demolition, we had to spend a lot of upfront time reviewing each job and making a custom plan. We would often make more mistakes because we were learning something new on each job. Once we started doing pool removals, we created a five-day process that ran like clockwork.

With the drafting company, the focus is simple drawings for permits. Fast, simple, and repeatable. It's easy to train new designers for the work, and the communication needed with customers is minimal. I'd much rather do 1,000 jobs at $150 each than do one job at $150,000. Now I prefer to never have a customer that makes up more than 1 percent of my gross revenue each year. I don't want to ever be beholden to any single customer; that's asking for headaches. Plus, when you work at a lower price point, things generally run more quickly and smoothly. If you need to refund an order, it's not going to put you out of business. If there's a payment issue, you can deal with it quickly. Finally, and importantly, a $150 job is much easier to sell (and continue selling) than a job for $150K.

Now, if you're doing $15 million per year, then the $150K projects make more sense. But always be careful about how much you rely on a single customer. I've seen brands destroyed because they decided to sell their products through a Big Box Retailer. After three years and having 80 percent of their business concentrated with one customer, The Big Box Retailer demanded pricing that would cut their profits out almost completely, leaving them dead in the water.

USE THE SYSTEMS

Once you put the right systems in place, a business that is profitable and repeatable takes care of itself.

Even complex businesses can be systematized to be repeatable; the process will simply take more time. The pool removal company had extremely complex systems and many moving parts. Several pieces of heavy equipment, tons of broken concrete and rebar to be removed, hundreds of tons of dirt to be imported and compacted, soils engineers, staff, permitting, inspections, and payments. The list went on. If one of these pieces was missing, the whole project stalled.

But once we had elegant systems that took care of each of these pieces, they ran like clockwork. Sure, things still break sometimes, but we have contingency plans built into the systems.

THINK LIKE A FRANCHISE

One of the best ways to know what is most profitable and repeatable for your company is to think like a franchise. All of my businesses could be made into franchises and run in multiple places across the country. The point here is not to create a franchise but to spot what is most duplicatable. Subway is the master of duplication. You can walk into any store across the country and have the exact same experience. Their systems and SOPs are so tight that these sandwich shops essentially run themselves.

Instead of being a General Contractor doing all types of construction, you might focus on building backyard in-law units, only remodeling bathrooms, or building custom outdoor BBQs. What exactly you focus on will depend on your business and what you've learned to date. Once you dial in on your niche and create airtight systems with predictable profit margins, it's time to rinse, repeat, and watch the money roll in while you sleep.

In some cases, you might need to find a path forward by doing what I did. Write a list of all the possible routes you could take. Run a Google Adwords or Facebook Ads campaign. Search for trends on the internet or social media. Go out and talk to people to find out the demand yourself.

Soon enough, you'll find yourself naturally flowing into what is most profitable and repeatable for you and your business. The key then is to create amazing systems around that one thing and stop wasting time on everything else.

CHAPTER 22

WALK AWAY

In my first business, if I didn't have anything to do, I'd drive to a jobsite, pick up a shovel and start digging with my crews. I had to be busy.

This was obviously not about output. In fact, being busy had nothing to do with how much I grew my business.

I realized how often I was busy for the sake of being busy when I had my accident and was limited to a hospital bed and my thoughts. I literally couldn't grab a shovel. I couldn't keep up the militaristic or cultural expectations any longer. And in the midst of that place, while I was looking for ways to keep my crews busy, I had the idea to run the Google Adwords campaign with fifty services I was capable of providing and found an overwhelming amount of clicks for swimming pool removal. So, I started marketing towards this specialty. It was clear that this was going to be the next phase of my business. Had I been out in the field laboring with my guys, I might not have found this niche that ultimately would save my business.

Of course, you don't need to face a near-death experience to realize just how beneficial time away from your business actually is. Each time you intentionally build rest and space into your life, your business will thank you. And so will your body, mind, and soul.

CLARITY AND CREATIVITY

Even before the accident, I had quite a bit of experience taking time away. I had already seen the benefits of doing so, just from a much different perspective.

As soon as I had the construction company up and running, I formed a ritual of taking off a couple of months during winter each year, when business would slow. I didn't want to lay my guys off, so I would leave and let them do the work that was available.

I'd jump on a plane and fly South. I'd land in Buenos Aires, Bogota, or Santiago and travel around freely for months, only checking in every time I found an internet cafe (this was the early 2000s). As long as there were no big emergencies, I'd continue my travels.

After 6-12 weeks, I'd jump on a plane and head home. When I got home, my job was to dig in and find out what failed. By walking away, I'd uncover all kinds of issues. Maybe I needed to establish the proper lines of credit, create hiring and management protocols for staff, or develop maintenance schedules along with protocols for truck breakdowns. But without seeing the issues, I would never know how to solve them. Every year, new issues would come up by my being away, and each year the business would inevitably grow stronger and stronger.

You can spend a fortune on consultants to give you an outsider's view of your business, or you can become an outsider. One of the big benefits of time away is clarity. You simply can't get this if you're constantly in go mode.

When you are in the thick of things, your judgment gets clouded. Think about the last fight you had with your significant other. Were you being objective and completely reasonable? Probably not. If people were able to be objective about things they truly cared about, many therapists and consultants would be out of work.

When you remove yourself from the day-to-day of your business and give yourself the space to look at it from the outside, you'll see what needs improvement. A lot of people who meditate understand this idea. Taking a break is a way to reclaim your space, learn, and reflect. After all, you can't read the label when you're stuck inside the jar.

Remember, you want to be the spectator—the coach seeing the full field of play. Some business owners see themselves as a quarterback, and therefore they're always in reaction mode. Even the best quarterback can only see from a single perspective. And when you respond only to what's right in front of you without seeing the whole picture, you limit yourself and your business.

Sure, you need some people in the business who can be reactive, but that's not you. You need to be proactive in each step you take. And you can only do this when you can see what's on the horizon.

When you see from this perspective, you can answer the bigger questions: when to hire more staff or what marketing directives will be needed to keep business flowing. You're no longer responding to issues like where to tow the broken-down truck or how to deal with an angry customer. No, you're the fat cat in the VIP box smoking a cigar and smiling because you see it all, and you know you're winning.

But clarity isn't the only benefit of stepping away from it all for a while. Something else magical takes place: you become much more creative.

Something I want my kids to know is boredom. Why? Not because I'm an evil parent but because I know that boredom leads to creativity. When you aren't constantly consumed by all the noise around you, your brain starts going in a whole new way.

By stepping away, you essentially tap into that childlike imagination that never actually left but only got overrun throughout life. You begin to see your business in new ways and come up with creative solutions you never would have otherwise.

Recently, another business owner emailed asking if I'd be willing to chat with him on my morning walk about his business. He explained how he felt like he was at a crossroads and wasn't sure what to do.

My response was as follows:

Hi!

My morning walks are by myself. It's when I get my head ready for the day. I've committed to finishing my day by noon, and that has forced me to be careful with my time.

I'd suggest you carve out an hour or two to walk every day. Leave your phone at home and think about the things you mentioned. You have the answers inside of you. You just need to create a quiet space to think them through. Give that a try for a couple weeks and let me know if it helps.

Ryan

To some people, this response might sound callous, but I am actually giving this business owner the best advice I know. Sure, there might be a time when consultation could help. But the truth is, even the best consultants can't help your business as much as you can. Only you know your business inside and out, and that's why only you can have the answers for it.

One of the best ways to tap into those answers is by simply stepping away. Start with a short walk, and see how powerful this space can be.

AN HONEST ASSESSMENT

I always hear small business owners say they can't walk away from their business or things will fall apart. But what happens when a family member passes away and they have to leave town for a funeral? What about when they get called into jury duty? Of course, in these cases, they figure it out.

The truth is that you can take time away, but you're scared. And perhaps for good reason. After all, if you take a half day off on Friday and things start breaking, your business needs a lot of work. But the fear is not a reason to not step away. Quite the opposite. It's a reason to do just that—so you can be honest about where you truly are.

Start small. Take every Friday off. Tell your staff that you have development calls all day and can't be disturbed. If you still get emergency calls from your staff, wait several hours to return them and see what happens. Did they figure it out? If you have the right people in place, they will always figure it out. And where there are still problems because of your absence, fill the gaps. Create better systems. Make that hire. Do what needs to be done so that your Friday is truly free.

Then take the next step. Take Monday off as well. Over time, your staff will get used to you coming into the office sporadically. They will also see that the business is thriving because you've set it up for success.

It's here—when you've truly reclaimed your time—that you'll start to see the real growth.

Most of my biggest gains in my businesses have come to me while I was salmon fishing on a charter boat or on a motorcycle ride across Alaska. My businesses were running for me, and I was reaping the rewards.

Stepping away is the way you put your new mindset and systems to the test. If you never walk away, you'll never know where you stand.

CHAPTER 23

TAKE TIME TO REFLECT

On July 3 each year, I set aside the whole day to reflect. I call this my "Alive Day."

The day is significant because I somehow survived an experience in which I likely had a 99 percent chance of dying. As I shared in the Introduction, the event altered everything for me. When I first woke up in the hospital bed, I immediately decided to stop smoking. That was, in essence, my first step in reflection. Of course, the reflection didn't end there. I also realized how I had essentially set up my life like a house of cards. Everything was surface level and could crumble. In short, I had settled, and I didn't want to settle anymore.

To this day, I continue to use this day to assess where I am in life and business.

PROACTIVE, NOT REACTIVE

One of the most important reasons to reflect is to continually ensure that you are not slipping back into reactivity or your old ways of operating.

If you follow everything I share in this book, you will experience this "other side of life." I have no doubt about that. The only issue is that it's all too easy to go backward. If there's one emergency in the business, you can quickly slip back into the workaholism you lived in for so long.

Workaholism is the other addiction no one likes to talk about, but it is one of the main addictions entrepreneurs deal with. They think they are being proactive by staying busy—or going back to being busy—but workaholics are actually acting out of a reactive state. They're chasing something more, something better, just like alcoholics and drug addicts try to do, but they never "get there." It's an endless cycle, and that's why I call it "The Hustle Trap." It's not easy to get out of it, but you must.

Workaholism, just like other addictions, impairs your connections to those you love and negatively impacts your mental and physical health.

Once you're out of the trap, you need to continually reflect to make sure you are remaining in a proactive state in life and business.

Part of this proactivity is acknowledgment and celebration. If you've scaled your business from 1 to 2 and have known true independence and autonomy, take time to acknowledge and celebrate what you've done. A lot of entrepreneurs want to just stay busy simply because they never look back and see how far they've already come.

If you've taken the small steps to get here, well done. Now keep taking those steps. That is how you continue on the proactive path. It's not about the huge gains that all happen at once. You may experience a few of those in your business, but the truth is day-to-day improvement is much more important for you and your business.

ASSESS YOUR LIFE ON THE OTHER SIDE

Are you living life the way you want to be living?

It's a simple question, and it's an important one to ask yourself on a regular basis. Is your life "on this side" what you actually want it to be? If it's not, or if any area could be improved, it's time to be honest about that and make the necessary changes.

We started the book by talking about you, the person, because your business all starts with you. It starts with your mindset. It starts with the effort you're willing to put in upfront. It starts with you taking full ownership.

Well, guess what? Your business also ends with you too. And if you aren't where you want to be, your business is going to suffer. So, take the time you need to reflect. And then be proactive in living the life you want to live. You've got this!

CONCLUSION

When the COVID lockdown started in 2020, I decided to start taking my health more seriously and strengthen my immune system. I applied the principles of my business to my health, focusing on data and constant improvement. I started a meal delivery service to ensure I was getting the proper nutrients. I wore a constant glucose monitor to understand my body's reaction to glucose. I wore an Oura ring to track my activity and sleep. I took Dexa scans to understand my body composition, and I tracked my weight, committing to daily walks and HITT training five times per week for 30 minutes. I constantly refined each of these over time and ultimately lost 50 pounds and felt better than I ever have.

On one of my morning walks (during the writing of this book), I was listening to a podcast on which the guest was talking about a whole-body MRI scan that can detect 500 different types of cancer and other things like aneurysms. It piqued my interest, so I paid the $2,500 and scheduled the scan.

To my surprise, the scan found a very large renal cell carcinoma on my kidney. I thought this couldn't be right since I felt amazing. I was doing better than ever, wasn't I?

I later came to find out this type of cancer doesn't generally present any symptoms until it's too late. If untreated, the cancer will get into your spine and pelvis, and there's little that can be done. My doctor told me if we had not discovered it, I would have been coming to him within the next year or two, and the conversation would have been much different.

Within a couple of months, I was able to undergo surgery and remove the cancerous kidney. And today, as I'm writing this, I'm cancer-free.

Why share this story with you? Because, for me, it sums up what this book is all about: *freedom*.

Had I been caught up in the day-to-day hustle of running my business, I would have never been able to focus the time and money needed to improve my health in the first place. I would still be 50 pounds overweight and lacking the energy I have now. I wouldn't have had the space to listen to a podcast about healthy living and almost certainly wouldn't have had the means to run the scan and find this tumor, which could have been terminal within a couple of years.

Here on the other side, I'm grateful for the years I have left to keep focusing on what truly matters.

For me, getting out of The Hustle Trap is about much more than building a successful business and making a lot of money. It is, of course, about those things too. But much more than that, it is about finding freedom and joy in all of life.

FIRST STEPS

I wrote this book to pass on what I've learned in life and business to others. The last thing I'd want is for you to get through it and then forget about the principles and never do anything with them.

So, I want to first encourage you to determine your first steps. Only you can know what those look like for you.

If you're just starting out, you likely want to focus on the principles shared in Part 1 of the book. It's time to frontload. It's time to take full ownership and know your business frontwards and backward. It's also time to take on a different mindset, an abundance mindset. Don't skip this step. Even if you are years into your business, you might still need to go back to some of these principles and make some changes.

If you find yourself drowning in the day-to-day tasks of your business, the best next step might come from Part 2 of the book—learning to find and leverage the right people. This is a big step for many business owners because it requires letting go. But the truth is you will never shift out of first gear if you don't take this step. Again, don't skip it! Go back to it if you are lacking people power in your business.

If you feel like you have the right people in place, but your business is still taking too much of your time (you aren't truly free yet), use the guidance in Part 3. Implement higher-level tactics and systems that will allow your business to work like that Black Box—on complete autopilot.

Finally, go back to Part 4 of the book whenever you want to be reminded of what life on the other side looks like and how to stay there and not slip back into your old ways.

No matter where you are in your journey, take that first step toward removing yourself from The Hustle Trap. I'll see you on the other side!

www.ingramcontent.com/pod-product-compliance
Lightning Source LLC
Chambersburg PA
CBHW031856200326
41597CB00012B/440